Ferreting F[...]
Upholding [...]

C000261119

by Simon Whitehead

all the best.
Simon Whitehead -

Published by Pakefield Ferrets

Distributed by Coch-y-Bonddu Books
Tel: 01654 702837
www.anglebooks.com

Published by:

Pakefield Ferrets
5 St Georges Rd
Pakefield
Suffolk
NR33 0JW
www.pakefieldferrets.co.uk

Printed by:

Leiston Press
Unit 1b
Masterlord Ind Est
Leiston
Suffolk
IP16 4JD

ISBN Number 0-9539337-1-7

Distributed by Coch-y-Bonddu Books
Tel: 01654 702837
www.anglebooks.com

Also available by the author-
Ferrets-Taking their work & welfare into the 21st century

Foreword

I am delighted that Simon Whitehead has written the sequel to "FERRETS- Taking their Work & Welfare into the 21st century"- until relatively recently, ferrets were field sports unsung heroes. Like the author and countless other people, my love of the countryside and the fascination of wildlife, blossomed when I acquired my first ferret as a small boy. In those days, available knowledge on ferrets and ferreting was largely by word of mouth and had hardly changed since they were introduced to these islands by the Normans.

A number of factors have catapulted ferret keeping into their rightful place beside hound, horse and hawk in the 21st century. Myxomatosis led to many ferrets being kept simply as pets and the discovery that ferrets are highly intelligent creatures who thrive on proper housing, considerate handling and exercise. Pet ownership here and increasingly in America, led to dramatic improvements in the whole conception of ferret housing, feeding and health, particularly reproduction. In my young day, a vasectomized hob or neutered jills were completely unheard of.

Rabbits were never completely wiped out and are now on the increase. Ferreting has long been recognized as the ideal way of introducing children to field sports and our role in the management of wildlife. Today, with our heritage and country traditions under threat from political bias and an urban dominated society, ferrets and ferreting have acquired a new significant role. Yesterday's ferreter is today's educationalist. Simon and fellow enthusiasts devote an enormous amount of time and energy at game fairs and county shows, helping young people interested in the countryside by providing expert advice on the practicalities and welfare of modern ferreting and ferret keeping.

Drawing on a lifetime's knowledge and love of the countryside, Simon has now written the definitive book. Immensely readable, it covers everything from health and welfare, to ferreting and the law, what equipment to buy and where to get it and how to set nets and operate an electronic ferret locator. There are instructions on killing and gutting rabbits and a selection of simple recipes.

Enormous care has been taken to cover every aspect of a day's ferreting, from clothing to the cautionary warning not to forget the mobile phone. I suspect that Simon's new book will soon be on every young countryman's bedside table.

Johnny Scott

Acknowledgements

To all the landowners, farmers and gamekeepers on whose land I have ferreted over the years, for without their permission where would we all go?

I am very grateful to the following for all their help in enabling me to write this book:

Nigel Housden for his time, advice and excellent photographs not only for this book but for all the material I have used for my articles and displays over the years. David Whitehead, for without his expertise on a computer, I hate to think what state I would be in? Deben Group Industries for there illustrations in the net making section, help and support to ensure the future of ferreting is easier on the ferret. Johnny Scott for writing the foreword to this book and to Eaglemoss Publications Ltd for their permission to use their rabbit warren and rabbit skull illustrations.

To Paul, a true countryman..

Last but not least, Jules, my Achilles heel.

Photographic & Illustration Credits.
Photographs and illustrations are the courtesy of the following:

Nigel Housden: pp. Front & back cover pictures, 2,3, 9, 14, 26, 40, 47, 52, 53, 57, 60, 62, 66, 67, 75, 76, 80, 84, 85, 90, 92, 95, 97, 98, 102, 104.
David Whitehead: pp. 27, 28
Simon Whitehead: pp. 43, 99
Paul Quagliana: pp. 7
©**Eaglemoss Publications Ltd, 2003**: pp. 46, 51
Simon Trinder, artist and countryman, for my ferret logo.
Deben Group Industries: pp. 77, 79, 80

Contents

Chapter 1

Introduction

Within the pages of this book I hope to give a sensible, no-nonsense approach to the traditional pastime of ferreting, and guidelines of where to easily purchase ferreting equipment – knowledge that I found hard to come by when starting out.

The methods and information covered in this book are not gospel, they are only advice as they will not suit everyone, but they have served me and my friends well over the years.

Getting to know your ferrets and equipment, coming to terms with the fact that you will get to know your spade well over the coming seasons, (like an old friend, some days you curse him or some days you cannot see him quick enough) is all information connected with purchasing ferreting equipment and something that is invaluable for the beginner.

Since the transformation from a smelly, aggressive animal frowned upon by many, the ferret is perceived as an animal that is as at ease in the field bolting rabbits to gracing homes across the world as a family pet. The mere fact that the ferret was more widely kept as a pet after the myxomatosis outbreak of 1953 played such an important role in the development of the ferret's welfare and something which we should never forget.

The ferret was domesticated for its role as a hunter, evicting (bolting) the rabbits from their underground warrens, but until recent years there weren't many good informative books or videos to help the beginner, only the word from the local warrener or ferret keeper.

It wasn't any different for me; my tutor was experience, both good and bad. Later on I was able to talk and listen to others; tips were often exchanged or sneakily forced out to make life a lot easier and therefore more enjoyable. To this day I am still continuing to learn more about ferrets and ferreting and if there is one thing that I have learnt over the years it is that there is no such person as an expert, only those who believe in their own minds that they are.

A ferreting friend of mine, Old Tom, hit the nail on the head when he said that ferreting was all about preparation, preparation, preparation.

Using the old traditional methods of ferreting, used by the warrener, keepers and ferreters of yesteryear, just adding that hint of modern technology makes not only the ferret's life easier but our own as well. Ferreting doesn't happen on its own like many imagine, a lot of preparation is needed to make the day run as trouble free as possible – the equipment, ferrets, and permission without which you won't be doing much except poaching.

Ferreting, that age-old traditional pastime, is once again popular because the rabbit population has hit the dizzy heights seen decades ago, but it is facing a new threat, deadlier than any legislation; this threat is an invisible one – society in the 21st century!

Never has the countryside, our green and pleasant land, seemed so far away. Too many are unable to taste the fruits it has to bear through its traditions and pastimes, because of fear. Fear that their children cannot go out alone, or with friends, to explore the countryside like we used to in our childhood because of drugs, perverts and political correctness. But without the youngsters and novices breaking through into ferreting, what will the future hold?

Every effort must be made to encourage children and adults alike to learn about ferreting

If we don't give them a chance or our help now, before it is too late, we have no one to blame but ourselves.

By putting together this guide to ferreting I hope to help lay the foundations of a prosperous future by enabling the ferreter, beginner or experienced, to enjoy their days ahead in the fields in pursuit of the rabbit. I for one am a ferreter who hasn't stopped learning since getting bitten by the ferreting bug many, many years ago, and I doubt I will ever stop learning.

Ferrets get everywhere!

Listed below are a few of the ferret terms that you will encounter in the chapters in this book.

Albino – ferret with pink eyes, coat may be different shades of white or cream

Bleeper – see ferret finder

Bolt, bolting and bolter – to evict, evicting and rabbit which has been evicted. Bolters sometimes refers to ferrets that will consistently shift rabbits, even the most stubborn one

Buck – male rabbit, also name for male ferret in different regions

Bolthole – annoying little exit holes of the warren, often hidden

Burrow – name of chambers that make up the warren, burrow or earth.

Bury – see warren

Business – collective name for a group of ferrets

Doe – female rabbit

Earth – See warren

Ferret – domesticated polecat

Ferreting – using ferrets to bolt rabbits

Ferret finder – a modern transmitter and receiver set used to find ferrets below the ground, comes in depths of 8 feet or 15 feet

Hob – a male ferret

Hobble – a castrated male ferret

Hoblet – a vasectomised male ferret

Jill – a female ferret

Killed under/below – rabbit killed underground by ferret

Kit – a young ferret aged 16 weeks or less

Liner – a hob ferret fitted with collar and line or ferret finder collar instead of line

Litter – family of kits from the same parents

Lurcher – dog usually associated with ferreting, a cross between a running dog (greyhound or whippet) and a herding dog (sheepdog) or terrier

Lying up – when a ferret has stopped working underground, usually behind a rabbit in one of their stops

Musk – strong scent produced by ferrets

Neck breaking – method of dispatching rabbits instantly and effectively

Polecat – common name for either wild polecat or a ferret with the markings of a wild polecat

Polecat ferret – a ferret with the markings of their wild cousin

Thumbing – to avoid tainting the meat of the rabbit, we use our thumb to extract the urine from the rabbit before gutting

Warren – name for the complex series of passages that are the home of the rabbit

Chapter 2

To ferret, first you need ferrets

The ferret has in recent years been transformed from a creature that was ridiculed along with its owner for being sharp, nasty and smelly, animals that were so misunderstood, often frowned upon by the misinformed.

Going by the descriptions above, you would think they were describing some sort of monster, not the ferret. "A smelly creature that bites when you go anywhere near it." "My granddad used to keep a couple of those hidden away at the bottom of the garden, we were never allowed near them in case we got bitten." These are the comments of many who used to see ferrets. But today the story is different.

Whilst I have been promoting ferrets and ferreting over the years around the country with my ferrets, there is one outstanding fact that has not only rooted firmly in my memory, but has spurred me on to continue writing about ferrets and in particular ferreting.

The thousands of people who I speak to each year, whatever their background, are all united by one major fact – their lack of knowledge of the ferret.

Go past the basic (and I mean *basic*) requirements and the majority struggle. I hoped I would never have to say this but I'm afraid it's true – whatever the ferret is to be used for, please remember that all ferrets are exactly the same, from your pampered pet to what this book is about – working your ferrets. Within this book I hope to answer the question of what, where, when and how to ferret.

Many people in today's society don't want to hear this but naturally we are hunters who through the ages have relied on hunting for our survival, if not we wouldn't be here today. This is one point we must all bear in mind.

The ferreter of old was an anonymous character, one who was seen but not heard. For some reason he struggled with the ferret. He had a carnivore, expertly adapted to hunting, a natural athlete, so why did he keep it in a small hutch and feed it bread and milk? As I said earlier mankind has a habit of fearing things we don't understand, but thankfully some tried to understand and this is where the breakthrough came. Instead of treating the ferret like a garden tool – only brought out when needed, kept locked away at the bottom of the garden and replaced when broken.

Today's ferret is not just a working animal but also a wonderful creature full of surprises and with endless enthusiasm that many animals would be proud of. This is why today it is also a popular family pet and as a working ferret which works its heart out as nature intended, giving countless memorable days out in the fields for its owners both young and old alike.

Like all animals they have needs, they need to be managed sensibly and properly. For any animal to work efficiently and effectively it needs to be mentally and physically fit, keen and ready for action. The days of neglect through ignorance are over. Education I believe is the way forward.

So to start ferreting you need a ferret!

If acquiring a ferret for the first time, there are some basic requirements you will need to know. Firstly never ever buy an animal on the spur of the moment. Whilst attending shows I see how people react to my ferrets. The vast majority automatically wants one.

That is why I don't agree with people selling ferrets at shows – who knows what fate has in store for the poor ferret? You must first find out the facts, both for and against keeping ferrets. What do you keep it in, feed it with and what care and demands does it have? These are all questions you need to know the answers to, so continue ferreting through these pages and hopefully your questions will be answered.

Firstly remember that a ferret can live up to and beyond eight years of age, and as their welfare improves so their life span extends – there is no magical recipe to keeping ferrets. No, I tell a lie, there is. And here it is.

Suitable accommodation, healthy diet, plenty of handling/socialisation and last but not least good breeding stock from which your kits will come. This recipe will ensure that not only do you have a contented ferret but that it will live with you to a ripe old age. Nothing could be simpler – so why do so many people struggle?

'Treat them mean to keep them keen'. This was unfortunately the norm in the old days. This gives food for thought to the image of old. This is the image that I, along with the rest of the nation of ferreters, want to help eradicate.

Ferrets come in many colours

So I hope that not only will the newcomer read and keep this book for reference in times of need but also the more experienced person who wishes to know a little bit more about the animal they have kept and worked for years or are about to keep, hopefully for years.

To get the best from your ferret you need to understand why it was domesticated in the first place to produce this fascinating creature we have today. As I am concerned about the future of the ferret so I will delve into the past only when I really need to, when it is truly relevant. I'll leave the historian's hat to the writers who are best suited to that particular subject.

The ferret, like all domestications before it, have been so for a reason – kept for enjoyment as a pet or used for working purposes. To domesticate an animal it needs to serve a purpose. But more importantly it needs a purpose to serve. In the ferret's case its purpose is hunting out rabbits from under the ground.

The polecat was seen as the perfect animal for man's need to combat the 'purpose for domestication' – the rabbit. This creature wasn't introduced to our shores until the Norman times, probably for food and fur for clothing for their troops.

The natives had heard of others overseas taming a wild beast to help catch this source of food in the hedgerows and woodlands of Europe as well as in the many large purpose-built warrens. There is some mystery as to which polecat the ferret is descended from; was it the Steppe or European? I think the latter but that is just my opinion. They are so closely related either one can crossbreed to another just the same as the ferret can to the polecat or, as it is often seen today, many will cross a ferret with a wild polecat.

Domestication was most probably reached by the usual method practised by many on the previous animals that have been domesticated by man. First they would capture young kits from these polecats and try to hand tame them, I say try because remember that these are wild animals at this stage and therefore share the characteristics of such animals.

After taming this beast they would then breed a captive male and female, handling the young until they had no fear of humans and therefore didn't see us as a threat to their food. Once this was achieved and generations of these animals had passed, a level of domestication was then maintained. Their social pecking order is then born, they have accepted that man is at the top of the food chain, relying on him for their food.

An animal trusts its owner, but like all animals, especially dogs, they need to be trained and not only for the animal's benefit for their acceptance into our way of life. A disruptive or destructive dog is a liability and the same applies to the ferret.

As the ferret spends most of its time underground the eyesight is not on top of its list of priorities and this is generally poor. The other senses making up for this are the sense of smell, and the hearing is acute. This is a point I exaggerate to the public to prevent them sticking their fingers into the ferret run.

To protect this bundle of senses we have a good fur coat, course hairs with a softer protective coat beneath it. The part of the ferret that most people remember is its mouth. A powerful set of sharp canine teeth.

When you take closer look at the ferret you will notice the elongated body, lean and muscular with short legs, the feet have sharp claws and pads under the sole of the foot. These claws are vital to the everyday activities of the ferret. If your run or hutch has a concrete floor or a hardwood floor this is sufficient when the animal scrapes to keep the claws down. Unfortunately the trend amongst some ferret owners is to clip these claws short, very short for show purposes. This only inhibits the animal; they are three-dimensional and need these for activities such as climbing and digging.

So there we have it, a brief insight into the ferret.

But what sex is best for you for working. Let us take a closer look at the differences between the sexes.

The jill (female) and the hob (male) differ considerably especially in the springtime when it is the mating season. The jill is smaller than the hob, with her head more streamlined as opposed to the pug head of the male, broader and more compact, and the body of the hob is usually about a third larger than the jill's. Lately the size of the hobs has increased, sometimes to a size too large to work comfortably with nets as they cannot pass through the mesh itself without being pursed like a rabbit would. For working the majority of ferreting folk prefer the jills as these are smaller and can easily pass through the nets and are nimble enough to squeeze into every nook and cranny of the warren as well as turning a stubborn rabbit into bolting.

Jill and hob ferrets – note the difference in size

9

Mentally the jills seem to have a better attitude to work, with that extra gear, as opposed to the hob that starts and finishes at the same pace. Some like this, but the majority prefer the jill because they can extend their ferreting family as she is capable of breeding.

One of the biggest changes that I have noticed has been how people are housing their ferrets. For whatever home you choose for your ferrets, that is their world. When not in our company this is all the ferret can see, play, eat and sleep in. So the least we can do is give them a respectful home, after all how would you like to live in the equivalent of some of the hutches the ferret has been forced to live in? Because of the basic knowledge of many a ferret keeper the ferret was, and in some cases still is, kept in ill designed and compact hutches.

Today, I believe we have a new breed of ferreter, a person who wants to learn more and know how to get the best from the ferret. When looking into what housing will be best suited to your needs as well as that of your animals there are a couple of facts that will have to be answered first. In the back of your mind you already know how many ferrets you are going to keep, perhaps with the scope for more. This is important when choosing your housing. You need to consider the space required for the housing, the cost and the design best suited not only the ferret but to you, after all it will be you who will be cleaning it out.

Let's remember that the world of your ferret revolves around its housing so make sure you take the time to make it the right one. After all how would you like to be cramped up all day and then be expected to be in peak physical and mental condition to perform whatever task is asked of you?

There are many different types of housing starting with hutches and going through to the ferret courts, with every conceivable modification in between. The three main factors to be considered with the housing are:

1. Shelter from the elements – in all seasons.
2. Suitably draught proof and dry sleeping quarters
3. Security – not only preventing the escape of the ferret but to stop rogue figures from taking the ferret out of their home.

The first option we will look at is the ferret hutch or cub, as it is traditionally known.

The most common mistake made by the newcomer is that they think that a rabbit hutch will be sufficient; they couldn't be further from the truth. Firstly ferrets are three-dimensional animals and therefore they need the area to satisfy not only the physical exercise needed to keep them fit but their mental requirements as well. Play plays an enormous part in the growth of the ferret as they learn their hunting techniques through play fighting and exploring pipes and so on. Not many rabbit hutches can give the ferret enough room to carry out these functions due to the design being for a rabbit, not the ferret. The hutch must be large enough to fulfil these needs. The hutch can be as large as you wish, but the minimum size should ideally be four feet by eighteen inches by eighteen inches and able to withstand this unpredictable climate we live in.

It needs to be designed to make the cleaning routine easy but more importantly secure enough to stop the ferret from escaping. The ferret is renowned for its ability to escape – a Houdini of the animal world. Times have changed since I first started to keep ferrets so I have seen how much of an improvement it has made to the ferret. The designs have changed as have the materials and the preservatives used to weatherproof the wood. The number of designs for your hutches are endless but your basic requirements will roughly be the same.

The material from which you will make your hutch has got to be practical, manageable and workable. Wood is the most commonly used and probably the most cost-effective option. Plastics are sometimes used but these tend to be expensive. Plywood or hardboard is ideal but I would not recommend using chipboard like some I have seen recently. Not only will it soak up any liquid like preservative or urine like ink on blotting paper, but will then degenerate and provide routes for escape.

The design should be so that the cleaning is made easy so you don't want a lot of gaps or obstructions, especially in the latrine corner. The hutch should preferably be screwed together for extra strength to the structure. It is up to you what design you decide but the main points are that the hutch is split into two separate compartments, the sleeping and the run.

The sleeping compartment must be solid, draught proof and have an entrance hole 5–7 cm round. This ensures that the sleeping quarters are dry, windproof and dark. In the summer this will enable the quarters to be cool with less bedding as opposed to the winter where the bedding is doubled for extra warmth.

The run section to your hutch should have a wire front to the door section which will let light and fresh air circulate freely, as well as a place for the water bottle to hang from. The floor is solid and secure with no ill-fitting joints. On top of the hutch the roof should overhang at an angle to let the rain safely wash away.

Another option for those who want a bigger living area but haven't got the floor space, is a wire run securely fixed underneath the standing hutch which will instantly double the space the ferret has access to but the standing space is the same.

When it comes to weatherproofing your hutch, again there are several important points to take into consideration. The materials with which you can preserve your hutch have changed for the better. You must use non-toxic preservatives and these are commonly found in any shop or store.

Creosote is poisonous to the ferret and under no circumstances should it be used. In days gone by paint was used, this is alright on the outside but if used on the inside, although it looks nice and clean the paint sweats and creates condensation thus wetting the inside of the hutch especially the sleeping quarters.
As you see in the photographs the roof should be at an angle, slightly overhanging at the front. The hinges and brackets used should be strong enough for the task ahead. Security should never be overlooked, not only might a rogue want your well-managed ferrets but also the opportunist thief might open the hutch out of curiosity. Padlocks are invaluable as they will deter many but nothing short of Fort Knox will keep your ferret 100% safe.

The position of your hutch is just as important as the design and building. The best made hutch in the world can and will succumb to the elements if positioned incorrectly. Make sure it is positioned in an area out of the direct wind and rain.

As you are responsible for the management of the hutch make the height at which it stands as comfortable to yourself and at a convenient height for you to carry out the cleaning.

As an improvement to the hutch some people fill the gap below with a wire cage & run securely fastened as this adds that extra bit of space for the benefit of the ferret. If this is done the floor must be either concrete or patio slabs.

One final thought on the position of your hutch, the seasons of the year change dramatically – there will be snow, ice and rain. Not only must the hutch be in a appropriate position it must also be easy to walk to because the last thing you want to do is to destroy your best lawn by continuously walking up and down in wet weather.

The second choice, the one which I prefer, is the ferret court.

The court system was the one preferred by the warreners of old because they could keep all their animals in one place. Not only did this make the management easier but also it gave the ferrets more room in which to exercise.

The court is a simple structure with the floor made of concrete or patio slabs. Some have used the more natural approach and used grass but this is impossible to keep clean, cuts up when wet and therefore gives the ferret health problems with constantly wet feet, as well as an easier escape route.

Those who have seen me at shows will know that I have a miniature court for my display team. This consists of a six feet square, four feet high court with a wire floor, which I cover with straw. But this is just for convenience because the ground on which shows are held are not always bowling greens.

Starting with the floor, this is concrete, either in block flooring or slabs. If slabs are to be used, please remember to fill the gaps between slabs with cement, as this will prevent any food or droppings being missed when cleaning. This is then not only easier to clean and disinfect but enables the ferret claws to be worn down naturally to a manageable level. On top of the floor we have the sides and roof of the court. Many materials can be used but the normal one is wood. The ideal size for this court would be 2m by 2m with a height of 2m. The height is important, as again it is you who has to clean it out and working in uncomfortable conditions can lead to bad backs and missed ferreting trips.

In many magazines and pet shops there are aviary panels for sale, these measure at 2m by 1m and are ideal as you can construct to whatever size you wish and know it will be well built. The best way of fastening is by bolts and then if you or your court has to move you simply unbolt the court and move.

One aspect of the court which many people overlook is the roof. Ferrets are three-dimensional creatures and although they are not as agile as the marten or mink they still love to climb, even to the height of six feet. A roof made of mesh is advisable unless you can ensure there are no gaps in which the occupant will find and escape but also to stop animals from getting in. Inside the court you can have branches, pipes and objects to keep the ferrets amused. A ferret with pipes, especially on different levels, will find the transition into ferreting a lot easier as it already is used to long narrow passageways at different heights and levels.

The ferrets can sleep either in warm, dry boxes inside the court or, like mine, inside a small shed joined onto the court with a section inside which is a little internal court with dustless shavings on the floor with plenty of boxes for the ferrets to sleep in.

A ferret court & ferret hutch with run underneath

Feeding your ferret
One of the biggest improvements in the welfare of ferrets is their diet. Never in the black hole of ferret history past and present has so much thought and consideration gone into the diets of our animals. This is so the ferret of the future can be a healthier and happier ferret.

In all the sporting and ferret magazines the subject of what and when to feed the ferret is a constant topic, with many of the so-called experts expressing such varying degrees of views it must seem frightening to the beginner, come to think of it to most ferreters. This is why it is important we look at the different foods, their advantages and disadvantages. After all it has been said that 'we are what we eat'. So why feed an inappropriate diet? This not only affects the immune system, smell and shortens the life span of the ferret but the general day-to-day well being of your animal. All these are considerations that you must make before deciding which food/foods are best suited for your situation.

The balance must be right as in all aspects of ferret keeping that is what this book is all about – building a wall brick by brick to keep the ignorance out of ferret keeping and ferreting.

Before, in the days when men were men and ferrets were frightening, the person who wanted to keep a ferret only had a handful of people to ask for advice about the welfare of the ferret. Sadly these were the types of people who did, and in some places still do, give ferrets a bad name.

There were few books about and these just contained the same limited information until the ferret revolution started. Books were appearing on the shelves containing logical and practical information on ferrets acquired through experience, looking at how the ferret was being kept and worked, realising that this way was wrong and sought to improve it – with great success. Year by year a new book would appear, building on the great start Fred J Taylor, Brian Plummer and so on had given to all of us in the first comprehensive books on ferrets and ferreting.

Don't be fooled though, these books were hailed by many as the ferret bibles of the times but, just like the bible, you have to read it and follow by example, but many of us don't. Don't get me wrong, I'm not a religious person – only where my ferrets and dogs are concerned.

This is where I feel the ferrets' feeding problems started. I'm not knocking the generations before me who kept ferrets because they didn't really know any different – the blind leading the blind. The problem nowadays is that nobody likes either to change or to admit they were wrong.

Today we look at welfare through a different pair of glasses, reactalights I think they are called. These are more focused than before and instead of being dazzled by new information we can look straight into it and make up our own minds. This is one of the areas where we have not only the few ferreters who blessed the pages of many sporting papers but the pet fraternity. I know it won't go down too well in some places, but be fair, credit where credit is due.

When myxomatosis hit our shores and there were no rabbits, there was no need for many to keep their ferrets. Wives, girlfriends and children alike were disheartened by the thought of so many ferrets being disposed of. Year by year they looked after their ferrets, not working them but just enjoying their companionship, wondering how to improve their lifestyle. Being carnivores, meat was the natural food for the ferret but what if you didn't work them and did not have a constant source of meat? Ferret keepers weren't satisfied with all the concoctions they were told of; to them this was just not good enough.

Dogs and cats I think proved to be the turning point. Natural carnivores, just like the ferret, they were being fed a mixed diet of meat-based biscuits, just like the captive mink were. Perhaps they thought this is the future.

The main ingredient to a long and happy life for any animal is a balanced diet, the right mixture of vitamins, proteins, minerals, etc. This not only prolongs the lifespan of the ferret but helps the job of replenishing all the effects of birth and stud duties that much easier.

The general misconception about ferrets and their feeding habits have stuck firmly for decades and these are still present today. Many people I see at fairs are still advocating the starving of ferrets believing this will make them work harder. The idea being that because the animal is hungry it will work its heart out ignoring the fact that it is hungry. This then leads to countless lay-ups because it is hungry and suggestions that the ferret is no good. I don't know about you but I work terribly on an empty stomach. If I saw a tasty meal would I ignore it? Of course not. So why do they expect the ferret to? I don't like sharp ferrets; I prefer to have my ferrets keen to work.

Over the years, after the initial myxy outbreak, the ferret began its transformation from a predominantly working animal to a pet and pet/working animal. For the first time the ferret was being observed closely by these pet owners as they had the time because the demand for rabbits became less and less. Not many people will agree but we have a huge debt to these early pet ferret owners regarding the dietary needs of the ferret. Without them who knows what stage we would be at now.

Cost and availability, these were at the top of their list when it came to feeding the ferret and these have a bigger bearing on the diet than anybody would care to admit. Ferret keepers of old had little understanding of the needs of the ferret; I suppose we are spoilt today because of all the time spent studying the old ways. But they didn't have the benefit of this so they started with a diet of bread and milk. These couldn't be a meal further from the ferrets' requirements could they? This was to be the basis of a legendary ferret myth.

An unsuitable diet consisting of mixed bread and milk resulted in an amazing increase in the smell of both animal and droppings which represented the equivalent of diarrhoea. The ferret then began to get the smelly image and because of the mixture of neglect in the handling and feeding the hungry ferret was a little bit more aggressive than a normal ferret of today's standards. This was their cry for help.

Then more and more keepers looked at its wild cousin for help and many things were discovered that changed how people fed their ferrets. The polecat, being a carnivore, fed on a rich and varied diet from amphibians up to large mammals such as rabbits. Meat had to be the main base of food, they thought, many feeding the complete rabbit to the ferret. This was great as rabbit contains everything from bones to fur for roughage. But their cleaning regime let then down and more often than not the rabbit was left in the small hutch for a week or so. In the summer it wasn't a pretty sight I can tell you. But everyone has to start somewhere.

Let's take a closer look at the foods available and how they affect the ferret. The health of a ferret and its diet can be judged by the state of its droppings (faeces). A ferret fed on a suitable diet should have dark, firm droppings with little odour. On the other hand a ferret fed on an unsuitable diet is the opposite – sloppy, light and very smelly – ugh.

The diet also has an effect on the life span; a ferret fed on a balanced healthy diet will live a longer and happier life.

Way back in time when I were a lad, all the ferreters I knew fed this milk slops with a little meat. I knew the ferret was a carnivore but what did I know? I was a newcomer to the big bad world of ferrets as it was then. But I was lucky; I learnt all about these ferret creatures from someone who had the best of both worlds – terrific working partners and excellent pets when not working. I saw both sides of the coin. Through the years I have seen many reflections of myself when I started and this, dare I say it, are the next generation of ferreters who will make a difference.

But why do we feed a ferret unsuitable food? Well nowadays there are no excuses, not like years gone by. Just take a look around the country fairs of today, ferrets everywhere. But only recently has this been the case. The ferreter of the past had no one to ask, no one to look to for good advice, only the shady characters of country folklore. Even these people were reluctant to give away what information might have been useful which is far cry from the pool of knowledge we all have at our disposal today. It is logical to say that the bigger the ferret the more food it will consume. But is it true?

The ferrets' feeding is governed by their metabolism, a high metabolism and the food is easily burnt off, a low one and it would be easy for the ferret to become fat and lazy. In the summertime less food is taken because it is converted to heat/energy. The ferret is less active in the summer but if the same amount of food was consumed as in the winter they would be likely to get overweight. The winter means that the body needs to convert its body heat from its food so more is consumed. The same can be said of expectant mothers or stud ferrets, storing fats for the coming birth and replacing what has been lost to the stresses and traumas of birth.

In the court system many ferrets that are kept together will establish a pecking order for food so a careful eye must be kept to ensure all are getting their fair share. Many believe in fasting the ferret for a day to recreate the past but I feel that as I wouldn't like to be starved for one day of the week then I won't practice it on my animals. The ferret court has always a bowl full of food in it in the summer and rabbit in it during the winter months.

The list below is of the more common meals that are being fed to ferrets, without touching on some of the ridiculous.

Water

This is the most important substance of all; without it we cannot survive. Water takes on an even more important role if your ferret is being fed a dry food diet. The water can be delivered three ways, two practically and one that courts disaster from the ferret.

The gravity fed drinking bottle. These come in a variety of sizes from small to large, usually made for rabbits.

The poultry drinker, available almost anywhere these are mostly used in courts where there are many ferrets housed together and the amount of water needed is substantial. This is more practical than having six or more drinking bottles around the court, but get one that has a lockable top to make it that little harder to turn over.

The drinking bowl, this was one of the earliest methods of supplying water, but taking into account the ferret's nature they kept being overturned.

Always check, maintain and fill the bottle/drinker regularly.

WARNING. Because water is essential, regular checks should be carried out to ensure the water is clean and free flowing. More care must be taken in the winter as frost can damage the drinking bottles. All drinking bottles must be cleaned out regularly to prevent a build up of algae which will give the ferrets upset stomachs if allowed to build up. To remove the algae from the bottles fill the bottle ¼ full with sand, add a little water and shake like mad. Rinse out all the contents and the bottle should be clean.

Food

On the food front the ferret has been fed a number of diets, some based on folklore, availability or what has been recommended.

Bread and milk slops

This was the first food for the unfortunate ferret. Not only was it totally devoid of any nutrients but also it gave the ferret scours (diarrhoea). This weakened the animal through malnutrition and shortened the average lifespan and is not to be recommended as a main source of food but can be altered slightly to provide a treat for your ferret. Add an egg to the bread and milk, cook and leave to cool. Ferrets love it.

Whole or part carcass diet

The feeding of the whole carcass to the ferrets has been carried out for years. This is the most ideal, natural meal for a carnivore such as the ferret, but the associated problems spurred the invention of the complete range of foods.

In an ideal world we would feed the ferret, it would eat up all of its food, no problem. In the real world the ferret eats a little at a time and stores the rest until such a time arises thus causing hygiene problems with diseases and fly problems. Husbandry has to be of a very high standard to combat this threat but more often than not it wasn't and the ferret began to smell and the rest is history as they say.

The same can be said of most meat. Pet mince is too fatty, dog meat has no nutrients and the ferret becomes tired and lethargic on such diets which are unsuitable for a long day's ferreting.

Feeding your ferrets rabbit has an unseen advantage and that is that they know what a rabbit smells and tastes like and this gives them that extra edge when working. Ferrets that have been totally fed on biscuit work the same but sometimes miss that rabbit in the dead end simply because it doesn't associate the fur with food. Nothing wrong in that, I know, but we must remember this when working them and you seem to be bolting less, it may not be your ferrets' fault.

Day old chicks

This is one of the more recent fashionable foods to hit our shores. Many feed these for two reasons, first they think because you are feeding a whole carcass the ferret is getting all the right balance needed in a staple diet and secondly they are cheap. For as little as 2p each they sound ideal. The down (fine feathers) on these birds is very fine and this builds up in the tract of the ferret causing infection. The bird itself having just surfaced from the egg feeding on the contents is low on calcium, protein and fat. This causes low bone growth in youngsters. However this food can be fed as a treat to adult ferrets occasionally.

Dog and cat foods

These are widespread and ferrets will eat them but care must be taken. The majority of these foods are deficient in the vitamin and mineral needs of the ferret so a substitute would have to be added. Cat food is slightly more acceptable because of the higher protein count but if regularly fed it must be combined with a bone meal powder (e37). This will ensure the right amount of calcium is consumed to help the animals' bones and teeth.

All of the fresh meat diets must be either fresh or thoroughly thawed to avoid poisoning the ferrets.

Complete foods

On the market today they are several ferret foods and although some are expensive they offer the ferret owner a way of not only reducing the smell of the ferrets droppings through a added deodoriser in the food but eliminates the threat of flies and because it is a biscuit it can be fed ad hoc and doesn't go off. This can be fed from weaning right through the life of the ferret. It can also be fed in conjunction with a little rabbit meat as is favoured by some. This is ideal in the warmer months, especially if you working long hours or have a friend looking after your stock.

Summary

There are many foods on the market. Feed what is best suited to your situation. It is the ferret that counts so cheap isn't always best. Look into your food carefully. Your ferret is your responsibility.

Ferrets that are worked have that little extra bit of keenness added when fed on rabbit as they know and associate what a rabbit is. This is often the difference between a few bolted rabbits and a few digs to get out further rabbits from the same warren. If the ferret cannot associate the two sometimes if the rabbit is hunched up in one of their stops the ferret either has very little interest in this ball of fur or ignores it completely. Some like this but when you are there to clear rabbits for a living this usually makes the difference between a few for sport or a lot professionally.

Ferreting is about bolting rabbits I know but some require professional results and this is a way of helping gain those results. Some call it digging as opposed to ferreting but when ferreting you should really gear yourself to get the maximum results from the performance of your ferrets, even if it means a few extra digs producing a lot of extra rabbits.

Caution

There are many foods which are potentially lethal to the ferret. These include sugar or sugar saturated foods, alcohol, human chocolate and nuts.

The ferret is a small animal so any treats must be fed in moderation. Many people like to give their ferret treats now and again. Please be careful and give healthy treats which will benefit the animal and not endanger its health.

Purchasing your ferret

The dilemma of purchasing a ferret, or any animal come to think of it, is one of the most underestimated aspects that has been looked into for the ferret keeper. I would like to promise that all ferreters have the same standards but I'm afraid I cannot. This is one of the reasons of this book being written, telling of the pitfalls you want to avoid – not written just for you but for the benefits of the ferret.

The ferrets' average lifespan is eight years so that is a very long time to correct a ferret that is fast becoming an unsuitable companion. That's why it is vital the right choice is made in the first place. Many a hopeful ferret keeper has been either put off or their enthusiasm dampened by the wrong choice.

But what is the hurry? There are ferrets everywhere looking for a stable, considerate home for the workers, pets or both. The one thing I cannot promise in this book is that you will not make a mistake. After all, the chances of me being there when you purchase the ferret are slim!

First of all the best age to get a ferret is when they are young (about 8 weeks of age) but some people prefer to obtain adults, and rescue and welfare societies are the perfect place to start if this is the case. Some are better than others but all share the pressures of countless careless owners who abandon their animals though lack of time/neglect, although in recent years the trend has changed.

The most popular and I believe the best time to acquire a ferret is when they are ready to leave their mother – about 7 to 8 weeks of age. Kits, as they are known, are available in the summer due to the ferrets breeding season and there are various ways of contacting people with ferrets for sale. First try the local rescue centres, read the adverts in the local papers or, better still, search the country shows. Nowadays at shows the ferret exhibitors on many stands will be willing to help you.

Never buy a ferret as a result of a spur of the moment decision.

Like all animals a lot of the ferret's attributes are carried in their genes. It is therefore important to take care when choosing stock. Don't be bullied or panicked into buying the first ferret you see. There are plenty more ferrets out there. Ask to see the parents, see them handled, where they live, the food they are fed, examine their stools. It is highly likely that some of the traits in the mother are going to be passed down to their young.

If you are happy with the parents and they are what you want, the next question is which colour and sex you require/prefer.

Let me put a myth to bed, the only difference between the many number of colours is the colour of their hair! This makes no difference to the character, working abilities or temperament. Only you will know what colour you prefer. The ferret has a wide range of colours ranging from the albino with pink eyes through to the dark polecat colouring. Some people think that there are two types of ferret, the albino and the polecat but as I said the only difference is their hair colouring.

Personally I prefer the polecat marked ferret, I think it has more character appeal because of the markings. But this is just my personal opinion. Albinos are easily seen in bushes and hedgerows so if working a lot of this terrain you may want to consider this as an option.

The next choices are what sex and how many. The problems they can bring if the wrong combination is chosen! For the novice, it is probably best keeping jills (females) together. It is best to keep more than one because they are a social animal and enjoy the company of others; this is a far cry from its cousin the polecat which lives in solitude. The combinations that could be chosen from are the following three:

1. Two jills
2. Two hobs
3. One hob and one jill

Two jills are probably the best combination, but remember in spring they come into season and they must be taken out of season. You could overcome this by having them neutered.

The two hobs would be fine until the spring when they come into season. They will then get aggressive towards each other. To overcome this you could get both hobs castrated, this will also reduce the smell of the ferret.

Keeping a natural pair together has the ultimate problem. Youngsters – and lots of them. When spring arrives, the hob will come into season before the jill. The jill will then come into season and if not separated, nature will take its course. Remember a litter can be up to and beyond 12 kits and these take a lot of looking after, feeding and finding homes for.

Be a responsible owner.

So, you have got a suitable hutch, know what food you need and have got it ready inside the hutch. You have travelled and finally you've brought home your kits.

Ferrets, especially young kits have plenty of character. This will develop as they grow up and will have a big bearing on how they will perform both in the field and as a pet.

There is one thing that stands the ferret out alone from other pets and that is you can NEVER handle, stroke, talk and play with a ferret enough. As they grow up several stages in their socialisation must be taken. The first and most important step is when the new ferret arrives. Leave them in their new surroundings for a while, perhaps overnight, as being taken from their home is a big wrench. Imagine for eight weeks living with a mother and nine brothers and sisters, having a party and then being pulled out, put in a carrying box and put in a big strange hutch. Yes, this is quite daunting so let the kits settle in before you start pulling them out to play with.

There are several ways of getting the ferret used to the hands; I will share with you the method which has worked successfully for me over the years. First you must know how to hold the ferret. There are some misconceptions which keep cropping up. The majority of ferrets do not bite. As I said earlier, if the parents are fed, handled and looked after well then there is little danger of your youngster becoming a biter; it is uncommon for a ferret being born a biter.

The character of both you and your ferret will be tested in the coming months. The main thing to remember is that this little ferret will not only mentally and physically grow quickly, so will its teeth and naturally, like puppies, they will want to explore with them. But with a cool, calm and collective attitude you can easily handle all the obstacles that might appear.

The voice is a tool that must be used. The ferret will get used to it and get excited at the prospect of you coming to get it out of its hutch into the big world outside its mesh front. Always talk to your ferret when handling, be calm and pick up in one swift action. Any animal has the capability of detecting the slightest hesitancy and tends to play on it. The ferret is no different.

A ferret that is both used to being handled and played with is a joy to own. The ferret thinks that every time you pick it up or approach the hutch it is an enjoyable experience and will gladly oblige. This is essential when wanting to work them.

There are two ways of picking up a ferret:

1. Pick up and hold the ferret like you would a cat. Talk, stroke and then pick up the ferret with your hand round the stomach, the ferret lying in the palm of you hand. This is fine if you know your ferret's attitude, but what happens if you are uncertain of the reaction of the ferret?

2. Pick the ferret up by putting your thumb and forefinger gently around the ferret's neck. This will give the ferret the security it craves but more importantly the ferret cannot turn around and, God forbid, bite you. This hold is useful when dealing with rescues!

If the ferret becomes restless or aggressive try swinging and stroking the back and stomach, this will calm the ferret to such an extent I have sent them to sleep in my hands at shows. If the ferret is pregnant extra caution is a must. Help the ferret's weight by holding around the neck and support the rest with your hand.

Practice these holds as much as you possibly can. Sometimes you come across a large hob and you may struggle to reach around his neck without strangling him. In these cases you will have to support him by his chest and neck.

Holding a ferret

Then progress this program by getting the ferrets used to the hands in all different situations, not just when picking them up out of their hutch. Put the ferrets on the ground and proceed to tickle them and rub their stomachs in an overplayful manner. This simulates the rough play of the mother and kits, which forms a background to their hunting skills if they were in the wild. As these kits have ever-growing teeth they want to explore everything with them.

Just like a puppy or kitten, you must discourage it and chastise it. The kit will go to nip you as it would its fellow kits, so it is perfectly natural. But what you must do is get the kit out of the habit of nipping you and start to teach it the difference between you, your hand and a fellow ferret kit. Over the course of the rough play, the ferret kit will nip. If it doesn't, good, but we want it to. How can we tell the ferret the difference and show it that hands are not on the menu, ever? That is where the rough play comes in – antagonise the ferret by this play, believe me it won't take much and w hen the kit strikes, so must you. *See photograph*

This is done by either pinching the nose or by flicking the nose with your finger. *See photographs*

To a small ferret kit this has the same impact as if we were hit over the head with a baseball bat.

Don't get me wrong it is not cruel and we are using the minimum of force. I don't know about you but I wouldn't need many hits to get the message. Every time after this exercise is carried out the kit should be rewarded when it has behaved itself. Make a fuss of it and feed it a titbit. Carry on this game until the ferret grows tired of it and refuses to even look at your fingers.

The next step is to place a drop of milk on your finger and let the ferret lick it all off. When the milk has disappeared the kit will examine your finger and more than often nip it. In the same way as before, chastise it. Your finger is yours and you need it. It is not on the menu. *See photograph*

With the continuation of these simple exercises each day add a stern "No" to the chastisement; this will reinforce to the ferret what is right and what is wrong.

The ferret kit's teeth are growing all the time, from birth up to about twenty weeks. This is a point worth remembering while acquiring a ferret for the first time. It is a lot easier to imprint and teach a small kit of eight weeks than a nearly full-grown 16-week-old ferret. The milk teeth of the young kits don't hurt whilst fully-grown sets are a different story, but also the brain is at the same stage. Remember the saying "You can't teach an old dog new tricks!"

Handle and play with your ferrets as much as possible and they will make being your friends and companions for the next six years or more that little bit more worthwhile. To successfully have a working career your ferret must be used to being picked up in a number of different ways in any situation that may arise whilst out ferreting.

Now you have your ferret, housed, handled and fed, so how and what do you need to clean up after it.

As surely as night follows day, the ferret's food is followed by the waste product – droppings. Cleaning is one of the most important tasks the ferret owner has to carry out. Although the ferret has an image of being a dirty, smelly animal, nothing could be further from the truth. Ferrets are clean animals, not only spending large amounts of time grooming but use the same toilet area time and time again. This is usually a corner furthest away from the nest area. This makes the cleaning easier. But what do I use?

Listed below are some of the essential utensils needed to clean your hutch/ court:

1. Dustpan and brush
2. Large bin liner
3. Scraper
4. Watering can
5. Disinfectant
6. Fresh shavings
7. Fresh bedding
8. A bottle of clean fresh drinking water

These tools should enable you to ensure that the ferret always has a clean and fresh home to live in. Because the ferret always uses the same toilet area, each morning/night just remove the droppings and sprinkle some fresh shavings. Check the water and replace if fully used.

At least once a week the premises should undergo a thorough clean and disinfecting. When using disinfectant make sure that it is ferret friendly, one easy way of testing this is if it turns the water milky white it isn't safe. The substance to avoid is Phenol. Whatever cleaning substance you use, stick to the instructions on the bottle. If the ferrets show any signs of discomfort, change it immediately.

Health, happiness, prosperity and general well being, this is the life we all hope for. So what is wrong with supplying this to the animals we keep and work? Many books and articles have been written about ferret welfare but little on how the beginner, or otherwise, can carry out practical ferret welfare.

Welfare is the subject that has completely changed not only the general conception of the ferret, but the way in which we keep these animals. Because we are human when a subject like this was raised, and people knew very little about it, it was scorned by many of the working fraternity of yesteryear in particular. This is when the ferret revolution truly kicked in. More and more ferreters were keeping them as pets as well as working animals when the dreaded myxy struck.

There was no need for the large numbers of ferrets to be kept post-myxy days, apart from the rat catchers, but some just could not bear to get rid of their animals that had given them years of pleasure. Enter the beginning of the pet ferret.

Ferrets were kept as pets for the younger generation, handled to the point of boredom. They were housed in large hutches, which dad was nagged to make and their diet studied more radically.

"Dad why is the ferret fed bread and milk when it is a carnivore?" was the norm. Only then did people start to look at the needs of the ferret. Don't get me wrong there has always been isolated pockets of people who fed the ferrets meat and cleaned up after them but these were rare.

As these children grew the knowledge grew and more adults were keeping ferrets as pets. Better housing and more research into the diet were going on and the whole welfare subject was gaining momentum. But was the old school listening? No!

I call them 'the old school' because in today's world the ferreter has more of a database to go to for information about ferrets than his predecessors did. This is often forgotten when we read in magazines week in week out about these so-called experts and their feeding regimes. Both the pet and working ferret keepers have their faults. Perhaps the pet owners are taking the term 'pet' to the extreme, the show people who clip, poke and prod may be a little too much, breeding ferrets for mutated hair length, exaggerated colours and sizes. Is this in the interest of the ferret? Well they think it is. Only time will tell.

But I, for one, have a fear for the future of the hunting gene inside our ferrets. If too many are bred out of these show stock, although nothing wrong in that, when worked a total lack of interest and eagerness is exhibited. Are they breeding out this gene and replacing it with looks, as in the spaniels, one for working and one for showing? I'll leave the answer to you, the readers. But just remember, you can show a working spaniel but just try to work a show spaniel!

Compare the two types of working ferreter. The old school ferreter keeps anything from a single ferret up to about fifty at any one time. Basic, very basic husbandry, fed poor diets or fed proper diets but not cleaned often enough. Cap this with "If you don't have a litter she'll die."

The modern ferreter is a proud person, not afraid to show people their love of ferrets with good stock, husbandry, diet and general welfare and when working the ferret comes first attitude – an attitude that is happening more these days.

Compare the two and reach your own conclusion. What do you want for your ferrets?

Ferreter number two has evolved through a mixture of seeing the condition of the pet ferret but also learning from the mistakes of the old school. These people do still exist I can assure you, old keepers, warreners and so-called pest controllers, all people who really should know better.

One of the most frequent questions I am asked at fairs is "Are they easy to keep?"

Looking at what it takes to keep a ferret happy, it doesn't take a lot. Keep them clean, dry and fed properly with plenty of socialisation. An easy task, so why do so many people struggle with it? What does it really take to keep a ferret happy? Plenty of handling and the daily cleaning of the latrine corner, water bottle checked and plenty of food. If fed meat, check for any food left over to prevent it going off, this is one area where the complete dry food has revolutionised the way we feed our ferrets.

As a rule the ferret is a hardy little creature that we have underestimated in the past despite their enormous appetite to please, despite generations of neglect.

As well as being the Houdini's of the animal world they can also be excellent actors as well. The ferret hides its health problems much the same as its wild cousin. This comes from its cousin because in the wild an animal that shows its weakness when ill is a target itself. This trait is annoying as sometimes the ferret is critically ill before anything is shown to be wrong.

Later on in this section I will go through the more common ailments that affect the ferret but first I will tackle the most talked about subject on ferrets.
Jill's – their breeding and seasons
We have all heard the tales of the old ferreter; "If I don't breed her she'll die." The same person then later moans that they are overrun with ferret kits. As time goes by, modern scientific means and methods mean we can deal with all sorts of problems. Because the ferret has become a popular pet vets are now seeing more and more thus gaining an understanding of the ferret. This we have utilised in

31

the ways we have on dealing with the ferret in season (oestrous).

As is the case with most animals, the season is governed by the expanding hours of daylight during the day (photoperiodism). The ferret, like the wild polecat, will come into season when the hours of daylight are greater than darkness. In the case of the polecat this is so the kits have the best possible start to life. Not only is it warm but also, because of the time of year, the mother will have a large supply of food to choose from. This is because all the other animals breeding have to explore the great outdoors.

We have now established that if the female ferret (jill) is not taken out of season, she will remain in season throughout the summer months and sometimes until as late as September.

To the novice this might sound a bit daunting, but believe me it isn't. When the jill is coming into season her vulva will swell up to the size of a peanut. If the jill is not taken out of season by whatever method her body will react to the female sex hormone oestrogen, which is continually sent racing around her body. If not acted upon finally this will cause a depression of all the three types of blood cells present. This can be potentially fatal in ferrets, if not the same year it could be the year after or later. If not removed from this cycle the ferret will not fulfil its expected lifespan.

On the other hand, I have known countless ferrets to live to a ripe old age without being removed from season. But there are always exceptions to the rules aren't there?

With the jill's forthcoming season, several factors appear to the owner:
Do I want to breed?
Am I ever going to breed?
Do I take her for a jab at the vets?
Is there a hoblet available?
If you are sure, I mean 100% sure, that you are not going to breed from your ferret the most practical option is neutering; jills will never need to be removed from season and the hobs won't fight, thus making the housing of hobs together easier. The accidental patter of tiny feet is avoided and the build up of aggression in the hobs is removed. Not only is the smell reduced but also the ferrets can be kept in any order sexually.

If you don't think that neutering is what you wish, or you might want to breed the jill, a jab or more natural hoblet might be the answer.

The jill jab is one of the more scientific ways of removing the jill from her season. Most vets are happy to administer this injection but it is always advisable to check. To most the jill jab is the most convenient method available. This is safe, cost effective and leaves the door open for breeding at a later time.

If you have a number of jills you might want to take the natural method. A hoblet is a male that has undergone a vasectomy. This operation usually costs around £30-40 from your vet. This little fellow can then carry out the service of taking the jill out of season for the rest of his life. He will therefore pay for himself many times over. This method is fast becoming a more popular option. People like the natural method because they don't like to fill their ferrets with unnecessary drugs.

When taking your jill out of season with a hoblet, because it is totally natural to the animals, a natural thing sometimes happens, well almost. Using a hoblet sometimes causes a phantom pregnancy (pseudo pregnancy). The jill will exhibit all the signs of the real thing; swelling teats, producing milk and nest making are all the signs but with one real difference. At the end of the 42 days she will think she has had a litter. Because I keep all my jills together if one of them has a phantom pregnancy they tend to think of each other as their babies. This can be annoying during the shows as they tend to drag each other back to the nest box all the time, however large the ferret is.

The jill will usually then come back into season in the summer and mate with the hoblet, the breeding season is then over and darkness outnumbers the daylight hours. The ferret will not then come back into season.

At this point I feel I must issue a warning concerning hoblets. As all animals can carry disease, the ferret is no different. The ferret can transmit Aleutians disease, flu and other diseases. It is irresponsible on the behalf of the ferret owner if they resist the temptation and knowingly loan a ferret to all and sundry knowing it has a problem. Tests can be made (for Aleutians disease) for peace of mind. The cost is minimal but the advantages are priceless.

Better cared for jills, fewer unwanted kits, especially for the overworked rescue and welfare societies but more importantly the future of ferrets will be a better place because of the chances the vets are getting to further their medical knowledge of the ferret.

If you want to breed your ferret, just like dog or racehorse breeders we all want to further our own line of animals and the ferret breeder is the same. Responsible ownership also includes responsible attitudes towards breeding and unleashing more unwanted kits into the world. You must be breeding for the right reasons.

As described earlier, the jill is coming into season, you want to breed and I assume you need new stock. Whatever reason for your breeding, the future of your ferret is at stake so the characteristics that will make up the basis of the ferrets are to be looked at seriously.

The stud ferret should be vetted thoroughly because a lot of your future ferret is in the father, e.g. colour, characteristics, size and workability. If like many you just want a pet ferret then the latter will be of no importance.

Remember, you know the ins and outs of your jill but if you are using another person's hob be 101% certain it is what you want and not just the first available hob. As with all animals if you want the best results put the best ingredients into the pot. Make a mental list of what you want and stick to it. Whatever the relations of the ferrets, whether it's line or cross breeding the results will be the same. So look, make up your mind and go for it.

Many different colours are obtainable through different crosses, too many in fact. I am not capable of, nor am I going to delve into the chasm of genetics over coloration; I think I'll leave that to the experts. The colour of your ferret is a personal choice whether it's a polecat or albino – remember that all ferrets are the same underneath. It's only the colour of its hair that is different.

The mating, in the animal kingdom, of ferrets is not a pretty sight. (Thankfully things are different in our world!) The whole procedure of the mating ferrets is a violent, noisy one. The jill totally submits herself to the hob; in return he drags her around by the neck until the mating is over. That's nature for you.

To have a successful mating the hob needs to be fertile and whilst this is normal you sometimes find the odd sterile hob. Although annoying for your breeding plans it could save the cost of a vasectomy operation. After the rough and ready mating ritual the pregnancy will last between 42 and 44 days. As the jill will use all of her health and strength during the pregnancy it is imperative that she gets a top quality diet.

As I tend to keep all my ferrets in a court I leave the jill inside this until 14 days before the birthing date when she is then placed in a separate hutch. This not only gives her time to get accustomed to the hutch but also to being alone. To some this is a greater shock than actually giving birth.

The birth usually consists of a litter of anything up to and beyond 12 but the average is between 6 and 10. The proud new mother will keep her little ones away from prying eyes for a while so unless you have a particularly good bond with your ferret I would advise giving her a little time to adjust to the kits. If you are worried and really need to see them, keep it to a minimum to avoid upsetting mother. You will have many anxieties if it is your first time but let me put your mind at rest. Ferrets have been giving birth for a long time and they're perfectly adapted to this job.

From when the kits are born you will hear their high-pitched squeals whilst feeding on mother's milk. At about three weeks they then start to take an interest in more solid foods. Mother brings the first food in so if you feed a dry food diet make sure the biscuit is soaked so the kits can nibble at it. Make sure if fed meat that you inspect and take away any surplus meat. Flies are a great nuisance at this time of year and it does not take a long time for meat to get fly born. The kits are now growing at an alarming rate so you will need constant food for them.

Between the third and the fifth week the eyes will start to open and this is the perfect time to start handling the kits. After plenty of handling and good food they will be weaned at six to eight weeks of age. When weaning, as with all animals, make it a slow process rather than risk emotional damage by just separating them all suddenly.

Ailments

The ferret is a bit of a hot potato where vets are concerned. Because they are a close relative to the wild polecat they tend to hide their health, as do their wild cousins, so by the time most realise something is amiss it is too late for the vet to do anything. Another reason for the lack of ferrets at the vets is that because they are so cheap people treat them like garden tools and when one is ill it is simply put down at home and a new one bought, just like a common garden spade. This behaviour still goes on but hopefully as time goes by this will become less and less, but at the end of the day it is up to the owner. Educate these people, and who knows. As the ferret is becoming more popular as a pet as well as a working animal the vet is seeing more of them. This in turn makes the ferret's life easier and also the charges for such treatments are coming down all the while.

The following sections on ailments are just a guide to them, not a bible of first aid. These are the more common ailments you will encounter, the list of ailments is a staggering one but that is not what this book is about, I'll leave that to the vets.

If your ferret is ill, or you think something is wrong, take it to a qualified vet straight away, remembering how the ferret masks its illnesses. If you delay it might go past a point where the vet can help.

So if in doubt - check it out.

The following selections of ailments are the most common ones you will, or may, encounter in the day-to-day care of a ferret. The ferret itself will need regular checks to see that everything is ok. In these checks you should look at the following points: feet/claws, eyes, skin/hair, ears and teeth.

Feet

The feet of the ferret are the most important feature, without them the ferret cannot walk. That is why it is important that we look after them and ensure nothing untoward happens. Foot rot was a common thing in years gone by but less of a problem today. The feet of the ferret being constantly kept in dirty and damp conditions produces it. This causes a mite to develop thus making the feet swell, scab and if not treated the claws will drop off – ouch. If you encounter this isolate the ferret at once, burn all the bedding and shavings and thoroughly disinfect the hutch. Seek veterinary advice urgently.

The claws of a ferret are non-retractable; these are situated on each of the five toes on each foot and can grow to an unmanageable level if not kept in check. That doesn't mean to say you must cut them back all the time though. If the ferret is kept on a concrete floor the claws will naturally be kept short, but they still might need clipping once as year. Ferrets on wooden floors will scratch the walls and floors to try to keep them down but again if the claws are too long and are inhibiting the free movement of the ferret they will need clipping.

The ferret's claw has a blood vessel inside the claw. This must not be cut into. The claw can be clipped to a sensible, comfortable length for the animal using dog claw clippers. Cut the claws one by one to an equal length. If at any time you accidentally cut into the vain use a bar of soap or Vaseline to stem the flow, this is to be rubbed in whilst the ferret is kept still to overcome the initial shock.

Eyes

On the occasion of the ferret's eyes having a problem you should remove the animal to a different cage (hospital cage) just in case it is conjunctivitis. This is easily treated with a solution of warm water just the same as it is for humans. Wash the eye gently using the solution, or gauze with the solution on it. Remember to discard the gauze after use. Sawdust, scratches and foreign bodies cause other eye problems. Again, care must be used whilst inspecting and cleaning the eye. When cleaning clean from the inside corner (near the ear) to the side of the eye nearest the nose.

Skin/hair

As with most animals with hair there are many things that need to be looked out for. Fleas and ticks are the number one pest of the ferret owner. There are several other complaints I have come across including mange and baldness.

Fleas

These are the one thing I can guarantee that you and your ferrets/dogs will get a visit from however clean your housing is. Fleas are contracted from other animals such as cats, dogs and of course rabbits, especially when ferreting. These can be treated by a number of products designed for cats and dogs.

NOTE: you will have to check and alter the dosage before treating your ferret. Ensure it is safe to use. Care must be taken if your ferret is pregnant or nursing young as there is a danger of poisoning the young. If fleas are encountered all bedding and shavings must be destroyed and the hutch/court disinfected.

Ticks

These are picked up in all sorts of places. Working ferrets usually pick them up around the head and neck regions. Ticks lay dormant and then wait for a host animal to feed on. Once fed they will appear bloated from the host's blood. These can be treated with a spray of the flea spray or alternatively dabbed with surgical spirits or alcohol. After a while they will shrivel up and die. Do not let them drop off naturally as they will only complete their lifecycle which will result in more ticks!

A number of good tick removers are on the market today but forget all those remedies of old. Burning off a tick with a lighted cigarette is simply courting disaster.

Hair loss
Nothing is more alarming than finding that your ferret is going bald in places. This could be down to too many eggs in their diet, excessive moulting or simply old age. Pregnant jills sometimes appear tatty and moth eaten but this will disappear later. Mange is another cause.

Mange is caused by an ectoparasite attacking the skin. This then lays its eggs under the skin thus causing irritation, scratching and the loss of hair. Foxes are the most common carriers but any animal can catch it. To humans it is called scabies. Seek vet advice if the animal is suspected to have mange.

Abscesses
An abscess is simply a wound that has filled with puss. Bites, infected stings or a foreign body puncturing the skin can cause these. When it developed it may go down with the aid of antibiotics or it may need lancing, sometimes both.

Ears
Many ferret owners clean the ferrets ears to rid them of earwax. This is often mistaken for the ear mites which infects the ears of ferrets and causes an irritation. The animal scratches uncontrollably at its ears and if left untreated the mite can enter the inner ear and this could lead to the death of the animal. The mite will cause a brown deposit with a slight smell. If you notice this then you could quickly administer drops yourself (drops for cats) or play safe and visit the vet. The ferret will naturally have a certain amount of earwax, this is needed to protect the inner ear but it is usually hidden from view.

Teeth
All animals, especially carnivores, have some sort of trouble with their teeth. The

ferret is no different and should have regular checks of the teeth. When carrying out these checks get your ferret used to having fingers in its mouth – your vet will thank you one day. Animals can suffer from abscesses of one kind or another. Some even clean the ferret's teeth with a smoker's toothpaste. A well-handled ferret should pose no problem having its teeth checked but if you come across a stubborn ferret a light pinch of the skin between the ears will suffice. What you feed your ferret can also affect its teeth. Some complete diets have a certain amount of gravy. This will stain the teeth and although not harming the ferret some owners might get worried when their prize and joy's teeth start turning brown for no apparent reason. Providing the ferret with a whole rabbit carcass diet or a carcass now and then will help the teeth by cleaning them whilst eating, plus the calcium of the bones is good for teeth and bones.

Heat-stroke
The ferret hasn't been designed to handle the heat so it cannot deal with high temperatures (would you with a fur coat like theirs?). Because they cannot sweat the only way of the ferret trying to cool itself is by panting – just like a dog. Strangely enough this used to be called the sweats. The ferret should never be put in a situation in which it is likely to suffer. Think carefully about the position of the hutch; never leave the ferret's box in a hot car. If you are showing your ferrets it might be a good idea to take a water bottle with a mister (just like you use for the plants) to cool the ferret down in the warm weather.

Use your common sense!

Aleutian disease
First discovered in the Aleutian strain of mink (hence the name). The disease is a parvovirus and attacks the immune system.
This disease can spread to all ferrets, parents to young, stranger to stranger. That is why it is important to take care in the breeding season and the removal of jills from oestrus.

This particular disease is spread from the fluids of the ferret, the urine and droppings, blood and saliva. Just like the spread of the common cold the saliva can be spread via the low volume mist emitted from the ferret's mouth while breathing, coughing or the dreaded sneezing. These mists can travel an incredible distance.

The symptoms of this disease, like many of the ferret, vary. Aggressiveness, fever, paralysis, loss of weight and dark tarry droppings are all signs that something is amiss, with death not far away. Unfortunately there is no specific treatment but the usual steroid and antibiotics will give temporary relief.

Diagnosis can be obtained by the usual method. A blood sample of the living animal can be obtained via a clipped toe, a deceased animal through a post-mortem.

In the eventuality of a ferret dying suddenly a post-mortem should always be carried out. This will not only detect any disease but also whether it is contagious. You have lost one you don't want to risk the others. If you have any ferrets that suffer from Aleutians, under no circumstances must they be bred from.

These are just a few of the more common ailments but remember: IF IN DOUBT CHECK IT OUT.

Chapter 3

Why ferrets and ferreting?

I sometimes wonder just what makes us do what we do. Why do some like cars or train spotting? Why are some destined to be doctors or politicians? And why do some of us like to get out in the fresh air in the countryside and recreate what our ancestors did out of necessity, and that is not only to catch food for the table but fulfilling their role as hunter gatherer and pest controller as well? Some I know are passing down these skills, from generation to generation; some are hooked at game fairs and their like; but some, like myself when I was a boy, are out of the blue fascinated with ferrets and ferreting.

Perhaps subconsciously I saw this happen on my travels as a boy on my push bike when bird watching or being somewhere I shouldn't, or I read about it in a book. I can't remember, but something inside me has given me the urge to learn, practice and fulfil this destiny. Perhaps this is what they mean by possessing the hunting gene!

This is how thousands of people from all walks of life, especially in urban areas, keep in touch with their roots in the countryside. Something that instinctively drives us to catch our food or control animals that are becoming a pest, or was it because I thought it was cool to keep ferrets, animals that everyone seemed to be afraid of? Today we can ferret with nets, gun, dog, hawk or any combination that the situation requires. But ferreting is an environmentally friendly form of pest control that ensures that not only are the fields reduced of rabbits but also there is good healthy meat for your disposal.

The history of both rabbit and ferret is deeply entwined, for without one the other wouldn't have been domesticated and so therefore created. When the Normans brought over the rabbits to this country large warrens were kept so the people had first class meat and fur to be used for clothing. They possibly used long nets to catch the rabbits fleeing from their warrens, I am not sure, but with the rabbit then in deep homes underground, called warrens, they needed a reliable animal to assist their harvest by evicting (bolting) the rabbit from under the ground for them to catch. Enter the ferret, domesticated from the polecat. Some of these rabbits escaped and shortly the whole island was infested with the wild rabbit.

The rabbit today is classed as a pest, in simple terms an animal that threatens our wealth or health and in the case of the rabbit, surprisingly both! A pest is simply an animal that is in the wrong place at the wrong time. Rabbits are fine in hutches but put them on the other side of the fence and they are a pest.

In 2001 vets found that an E.coli outbreak in Norfolk was caused by wild rabbits picking up the virus from cattle dung in the surrounding fields and travelling into a wildlife park, therefore spreading a potentially lethal virus to the humans on site. Only 12 were affected.

So serious was the scare that the Department for the Environment at the time warned that every time in the future there is an outbreak they will have to look at the rabbits, whereas in the past they have not.

So you see the rabbit not only causes millions of pounds worth of damage to the land but also has the potential to transmit disease as well. But it wasn't always that way.

The Normans introduced the rabbit to these shores, not only as a valuable source of food but for their fur as well. Rabbit meat was, and still is, a meal that can offer a higher percentage of protein with less fat than pork, chicken, lamb or beef. Add to this the potential use of the fur for protection and this made the rabbit a valuable commodity.

It was not long before people caught on and many landowners and estates had developed and kept huge warrens of rabbits purely for food and clothing. The people who looked after the rabbits were called warreners, a name that will stick with the rabbiter for life.

The rabbit numbers kept rising and rising until, in the 1800s, they became a pest to the ever-growing agricultural scene. More and more damage was being reported so the government had to do something. Various laws were brought in to combat the rising numbers. As previously rabbiting was confined to the noble few, punishment for poaching was severe (does Australia ring a bell?) but a new law, the Ground Game Act, made it possible for any tenant to hunt the rabbit. By the turn of the 20th century up to 100 million rabbits were caught annually.

The Government was so concerned that they drafted in extra laws to designate the whole of England and Wales a rabbit clearance area, giving all an obligation to control rabbits on their own land. During 1950 rabbit damage cost a staggering £50 million.

As the Government was discussing how to control the numbers a disease was hitting our shores in the south that would change the nation's perception of the rabbit and ferret forever – myxomatosis, a man-made disease that was developed on the continent to control the millions of rabbits.

Rabbit with myxomatosis

The rabbit flea carries the disease, so spreading from wild to domestic rabbits is not a problem, that is why the virus is most dangerous when the rabbits are all underground in cold or severe weather.

This flea was thought to have been carried by birds coming over from France and it found a native rabbit. The rabbit succumbs to the disease and the ears, eyes and bottom swell, emitting a bright puss.

During 1953-54 the numbers dwindled down to just 1% of the previous year. Yes 99% of all rabbits had perished. A slow and very painful death.

The saviour, strangely, was the runts and outcasts of the warrens. These rabbits were forced to live outside the warrens above ground, away from the rabbit flea-infested burrows.

Slowly the rabbit hit back, the strains of myxomatosis were getting weaker by the year, and by the 1970s the rabbit numbers were becoming immune to myxomatosis in some areas.

Today there is a new disease that is threatening to wipe out the rabbit once more. V.H.D. Rabbit Viral Haemorrhagic Disease has been recorded in the U.K. in the 90s. This disease takes 1 to 2 days from start to finish with the animal dying in a fit condition, unlike myxomatosis. It has been feared that this would spread like myxomatosis but until now it has only had local sporadic outbreaks. Rabbits in the U. K. seem to have a certain amount of luck to thank for this. For this disease to spread it has to be passed by spray, blood, etc. With the whole cycle taking a fast 48 hours the rabbits don't have time to travel to infect other areas, they don't have a flea to lay dormant waiting for its next victim, so you see it may be a victim of its own efficiently.

Today it has been estimated that the rabbit damage annually is over £100 million a year with the potential to double. Because the rabbit numbers were rising the interest in the control of them rose again and ferrets and lurchers were popular once more.

When we start to control an animal we first must understand how it lives and where we can find it.

The male rabbit is known as a buck with the female a doe. The male can weigh between one and two kilos and in turn it can eat up to 25% of its body weight of greens per day. As with all animals the female is smaller and more petite than the male.

These animals usually breed from January until August but with more and more mild winters we are experiencing births all year round. The early born can reproduce at 4 months of age. Having a gestation period of 28 to 30 days it has been calculated that in perfect conditions a doe having 5 litters a year containing 5 youngsters could be responsible for more than a million rabbits in three years. I know the chance of this is slim but it just shows why the rabbit has a reputation for being a sexually orientated animal.

Some say that if you get all the wild animals on one side of the scales you could equal the balance with just the rabbit population on the other side. How true this is I don't know.

The young are not only born in the main warren but in stops, a tunnel of about three feet long. The young are inside with the end sealed. Mother comes once daily to suckle the young until weaned at 21 to 28 days old.

Over 90% of rabbits die before their first year is over, most of these within the first three months.

So when you are surveying the area, if you see plenty of really young rabbits it is a good chance that it is not the main warren, just a nursery. Rabbits live in a system of tunnels called burrows and these, when connected, are a warren. The warren may consist of anything from 2 to 200 entrances and more and filled with many networks of tunnels and botholes. This is the area for the ferret to do its work.

Rabbits then move from this safe haven to search for food. The more rabbits in a colony the greater amount of food will be consumed in the area. A rabbit may have to travel a field or two for good nutritional food and they can re-colonise at an alarming rate.

Before you embark on your day's ferreting you need to do a survey of the area, to see the areas of damage, where the warrens are and also the safe and not so safe areas to work.

The rabbit can inflict a large amount of damage; there are not many crops or cereals that these little creatures don't have a taste for. It has been calculated that on a field of winter wheat the rabbit can inflict a 1% yield loss per hectare – that is a staggering 65 kg of wheat per rabbit. This is based on the number of ears lost and the loss of grain per ear. In recent years the amount of oilseed rape that the rabbits have added to their menu is catastrophic for the farmer.

But to go ferreting, apart from your ferrets and equipment, you need rabbits. Take a look around and watch out for the tell-tale signs – rabbit scrapes, runs and droppings; look at night with a powerful lamp. Ask locals for their knowledge of the land especially people who work on or near it. And look for damage to crops, buildings and forestry. All tips and skills you will pick up with time. But don't let your mind be confused where the rabbit population shares land with deer. You can tell the difference between deer and rabbit damage by the teeth marks on the trees and branches. The rabbit has both upper and lower incisors that cut a smooth 45 degree cut whereas the deer lacks the upper incisors so therefore leaves a ragged edge to the top edge of their cut.

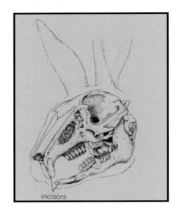

Rabbit's skull showing expertly adapted teeth

But beware; it is not just rabbits that will eat the edges of the farmer's crops! A lot of people mistake the damage caused, especially around ponds and water, by moorhen and coot. This looks like rabbit damage, but isn't. As the numbers of these birds rise, so does the damage, I have seen many farmers who would swear blind it is rabbit damage but it isn't, and until we have shown them no holes but plenty of birds in his fields have they relented.

Just because you see a certain amount of rabbits in one field doesn't necessarily mean that is the place where they live.

Find the hot spots and try deal with them first, don't be fooled by looking at a lot of holes thinking that they all join, you'll be surprised. Try to resist just ferreting the easy warrens, the hardest tend to hold the most rabbits as they feel safer, protected from danger in such places – but only if you have the experience, confidence and necessary equipment.

Because laws, especially concerning the rabbit, govern everything so there are certain laws affect ferreting, some directly some indirectly.

Rabbit damage in an orchard

Young rabbits cause damage too!

Know your rights – ferreting and the law

When you are working your ferrets there are a number of laws that may help or hinder you. These laws not only affect how your animals are kept but also how you treat your quarry, the rabbit.

These laws are there for everyone to look at and use but not enough people actually take the time to use them. These laws are an excellent bargaining point when approaching a farmer or landowner about controlling rabbits on their land or explaining to a stranger just what you are doing and why you are doing it.

You will not only gain respect but probably more permission in the process if you show a professional attitude whilst going about your business. Remember every time you go out it is the whole of country sports you are representing not just yourself!

Pest Act 1954
Rabbit Clearance Orders (Under Section 1)
Rabbit Clearance Order no. 148 issued in 1972 made the whole of England and Wales a rabbit clearance area (excluding the city of London, the Isles of Scilly and Skokholm Island).

Occupiers Responsibilities in Rabbit Clearance Area (Under Section 1)
All occupiers have a continuing obligation to control rabbits living on, or resorting to, their land unless they can establish that it is not reasonably practicable for them to do so, when they must prevent the rabbits from doing damage, e.g. by fencing them in with rabbit-proof fencing. Local Authorities have an obligation to control rabbits on their own land.

An occupier within a rabbit clearance area has unrestricted rights to kill rabbits on his land by any lawful means except by shooting.

Spread of myxomatosis (Under Section 12)
It is illegal to use an infected rabbit to spread myxomatosis.

The Wild Mammals (Protection) Act 1996
This Act plugs a loophole that existed in wildlife legislation, where non-captive wild animals had little or no protection. It made it an offence to: mutilate, kick, beat, impale, stab, burn, stone, crush, drown, drag or asphyxiate any wild animal

with intent to inflict unnecessary suffering.

Exceptions allow pest control, shooting, hunting and coursing to be carried out providing that the animal is killed swiftly. This eliminates drowning as a means of dispatching trapped animals.

Agriculture Act 1947

Under Section 98 any person having the right to do so may, by written notice, be required by the Minister to take such steps as may be necessary for the killing, taking or destruction of certain animals or birds (or their eggs) for the purpose of preventing damage to crops, pasture, animal or human foodstuffs, livestock, trees, hedges, banks or any works on land. The notice may specify time limits for any action, the steps to be taken and the land on which they are to be taken.

Animals that may be specified in the notice are rabbits, hares, other rodents, deer, foxes and moles. There are powers to add other animals to the list. The birds that may be specified are all wild birds not protected by Schedule 1 or the Wildlife and Countryside Act 1981. Under Section 98 (7) (added by Section 2 of the Pests Act 1954) an occupier may be required by written notice to destroy or reduce breeding places or cover (e.g. scrub) for rabbits or to prevent rabbits from spreading or doing damage elsewhere.

Under Section 99 occupiers of land may be required to take steps to prevent the escape of animals from land on which they are kept in captivity, but only if the animals are agricultural pests or animals which might damage banks or land-works. Dangerous animals are not included – they are the responsibility of local authorities.

At the time of writing the Countryside Right Of Way Act (C.R.O.W) is in process. This has the potential to cause a lot of grief to the ferreter, giving people the right of way to private land, land which you might be ferreting. Keep an eye out for this one in the future!

It is essential that to carry out your ferreting, and you do have the law on your side, you must first find the home of the rabbit, the warren. This can be situated in all sorts of positions usually in the least accessible part of the field, but not always. Just because a field has a lot of rabbits feeding does not necessarily mean they live there. The same can be said of holes, just because there are holes on the side of the field doesn't necessarily mean they are always occupied. The rabbit is a fiercely territorial animal, far from its image – a cute cuddly animal that will harm nothing. The rabbit can cover a field or two in search for quality food and often does so.

Having carried out your surveillance you will hopefully have spotted the following: crop damage – droppings – the rabbits in the field – scrapes and rabbit runs – entrance or boltholes from the warren and the warren itself.

All signal the presence of the rabbit, but it is the warren that we are interested in. These can vary from anything from a simple two-hole to a complex and ancient warren with a couple of hundred holes. Before you use your ferrets on new land this sort if surveillance is a necessity. Ignore this advice and you will follow the fate of many a ferreter who thought they knew best.

Like a lot in ferreting, experience will teach you a great deal when preparing to use your ferrets. Listen to all the help and information and in time you will decide which will suit you best. No two rabbit warrens are the same; indeed, nothing when dealing with nature is the same twice in a row.

It doesn't take a lot of rabbits to damage the land. There may be as many as up to five times the amount of rabbits seen on the land actually living/feeding on that land. Rabbits cause all sorts of damage, from livestock grazing to crops so it is vital that the warren complex is understood properly.

As you can see the warren is made up of a series of tunnels, both free flowing and ones with stops in. Mounds of earth excavated from the warren usually signal the main entrances to the warren.

This is the place for your ferrets to work. Understanding how the rabbit lives will help you overcome the problems they can cause you on a day's ferreting – spotting those annoying boltholes, how many ferrets to work the warren and spotting the rabbits living above ground and sending them below before ferreting starts.

As you can see the rabbit needs to be controlled, and today controlled within our laws. If there were not a need for the rabbit to be controlled, the ferret would never have been domesticated in the first place. As a ferreter you are simply using what we have adapted from nature to help control the rabbit population in an environmentally friendly way.

The rabbit warren

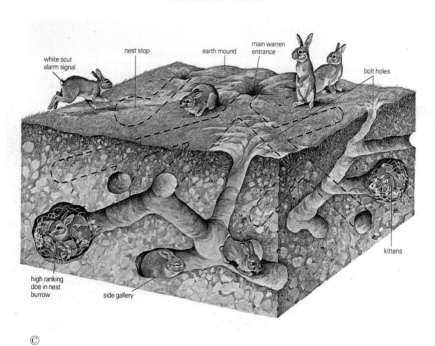

white scut
alarm signal

nest stop

earth mound

main warren
entrance

bolt holes

kittens

high ranking
doe in nest
burrow

side gallery

©

Elle

Paul - a true countryman

Chapter 4

Equipment – what you need to get started

Ferrets can be worked in a number of ways, most combining in one way or another. You can work with nets, with dog, with hawk or shoot over the ferrets. The number of combinations is numerous so I will keep it simple, but there is one point I would like to make – never work your ferret without a ferret finder – why go to all the trouble of rearing and training a ferret and have all the equipment just to lose your ferret because you had no way of telling where it was in case something didn't go to plan. It might only be six inches away from you, but more of that later.

First I will go into the equipment that you will need for any ferreting trip.

The beginner's ferreting kit bag

The magical quality of ferreting is that you can start with the barest of kit and keep with it or expand as your needs and ferreting team does. The starter's pack consists of the essentials to begin with. A couple of ferrets, a good box to carry them about in, some permission to work them, some nets to catch the rabbits (twenty is a good number to start with) a ferret finder set with a couple of collars to find your ferrets if anything goes amiss, a good weatherproof bag for your equipment and of course a spade to retrieve both ferret and rabbit with.

Equipment to get you going

This may expand but more of that later, for now let's deal with the basics.

Getting your permission to ferret

The first and most vital piece of equipment is your permission for without it you won't be going hunting. Gaining ferreting permission can be very hard to begin with, but be determined and prepared to take the lows with the highs.

Your first port of call should be any of the local ferreters that you or your friends may know. During my time promoting ferreting at shows I got overwhelmed by the number of young, would-be ferreters who just cannot get a break. I believe education is the way to save our pastimes but how can we teach people when they are not allowed the land to learn on? People are suspicious about would-be ferreters as they have been caught out before – promises of good timekeeping and reliability all go down the pan when the weather turns bad. Once bitten twice shy – so show them you can be reliable and trustworthy.

Become a member of the one of the major organisations such as the Countryside Alliance, BASC or the Union of Country Sports Workers (U.C.S.W.) and ask their regional office for local contacts. I mention joining one of these organisations as every person who participates in any country sport, ferreting or otherwise, should be a member. Not only do they offer excellent insurance packages but I find that they are essential when seeking permission for the first time and also they are the organisations at the forefront in the battle to ensure we keep ferreting for many years to come.

We live in an age of misunderstanding and the many that misunderstand our way of life are constantly trying to banish it to the history books. We have a freedom of choice, a choice to participate in legal sports and we intend to keep it that way.

Trying to gain permission today is a lot different from say 10/20 years ago. Many farmers have had their vision of the ferreter blighted by the not so thoughtful people in the past. Be vigilant; target the local farmers and gamekeepers or local shooting clubs. Wildfowling or shooting clubs usually have many different sorts, usually one or two ferreters amongst them. But occasionally you will encounter some farmers or landowners whose mood changes with the weather and you will have to play the mood, some get it right first time, some don't.

When you have go to make an appointment beware – FIRST IMPRESSIONS COUNT. Wear smart, respectable clothes, clean your car, and don't go in your work or ferreting clothes as you can look as if you came from the local tramp colony.

Point out the advantages you can provide and perhaps, in the case of keepers, offer your services for beating. Point out the areas of rabbit damage and offer your services. Once you have gained permission word often spreads like wildfire.

Pick those areas that are being damaged and do those first, the hard to get at warrens will most certainly harbour the most rabbits and this will be noticed and leave the easy warrens for your icing on the cake. Many just ferret the easy warrens and simply ignore the harder ones; they all need doing so do the job properly.

This is how I started many moons ago, helping a local dairy farmer. When the farm disbanded I searched for another place to ferret. As the ferrets were worked the word spread, I was persistent to the point of annoyance. I now find that I have too much permission to sensibly ferret. This I try to pass on to other ferreters, but beware, for they are not all what they seem.

Your reputation is at risk if you give permission (reputations can take years to build and be undone in minutes) without notifying or asking the permission of the landowner/farmers because if in any way the farmer is under the illusion it is you who is controlling the rabbits, anything could happen, and you could find yourself in the same position as the following ferreter.

Due to the amount of land needing controlling the permission was to be shared. Both had areas to control so there was no need to cross onto each other's patch. Imagine the horror at the local clay shoot for the original ferreter to be told of someone rabbiting on the patch he was about to do. So he went to investigate. Large deep holes were left unfilled; nets were left set on holes near a footpath. What a nightmare.

It took many phone calls and meetings not only to convince the landowner that it wasn't the original person but also to keep the permission itself. So be warned. This is, sadly, a common tale of why it is so hard to get permission in the first place. It is your duty to convince and promise that you will do everything in your power to leave the land in the state that you found it and if you are suspicious of any damage to gates and fencing etc, to report it.

Its better to be safe than sorry, that is why I prefer to get my permission in writing so I can prove to anyone that I do have permission to be there other than wasting a good ferreting day in travelling to see the farmer or ringing him up in the middle of his dinner.

Ferreting has a magical quality about it; it is a pastime that can be as cheap or expensive as you make it. For the beginner the basics will be few but these will grow in time – and they will.

How many ferrets does it take to ferret a warren?
Now we can take a look at the ferrets and how many you may or may not need. Then once you know, you will need something to carry them about in, a ferret finder set, some nets, a spade and probe, to start with. But let's take a look at the ferrets first.

Once you have gained either permission or a ferreter to show you the ropes, so to speak, you will need ferrets to ferret with, that's the object of this book – but how many?

One of the beauties of ferreting is the mysterious nature of the rabbit. No two warrens are the same; no two situations are the same. The rabbit's reactions in the same place but at different times vary. It's just so unpredictable.

So how many ferrets will you need to bolt these rabbits?

The ferret puts in an immense amount of work during a day's hunt and this is often overlooked. A tired ferret tends to struggle and more than often ends up in a lie up resulting in an unwanted dig. Ensure you have enough ferrets for the amount of work planned for the day as the size of the warren that is to be worked will dictate just how many ferrets should or could be used.

Imagine the rabbit warren as a car park, some small, and some large multi-storeys on a single level or on many levels, some with a single exit/entrance or some with four or five. Just for a second try to imagine the trouble you would have trying to find a car that is on a five level car park, especially as the owner has forgotten to tell you where it is, just that it is a certain car/colour. Hard isn't it? But if you had four mates and split up, well life would be a lot easier and the job done more efficiently. But on the other hand if you and your four mates were on a single level 40-space car park you would be tripping over each other. To an extent the same applies to ferrets. If entered in a large warren a single ferret would find it hard to bolt any rabbits because the single ferret is insufficient to force them out, whereas four or five can work the levels and force the rabbit to see that life outside is a better option. But put the same number in a small warren and the rabbit is trapped, unable to find a stop end or bolt. It finds itself with a ferret to the front and rear – result, a single bite to the base of the skull and a dead rabbit along with a potential for trapping the other ferrets behind it. But as your knowledge and experience grow, you will know what and what not to do. This is the trap many fall into and blame their ferrets for being no good when that poor single ferret had to tackle an extremely large warren on its own.

Look how the albino ferret stands out and is easily seen

If you only have a couple of ferrets, try to pace your ferrets and of course, yourself. For the majority of trips four ferrets is ample, two for the smaller ones. The bigger the warrens and amount of warrens worked in a day also has a big bearing on the number of ferrets needed. A warrener I know on the local estate can use up to fifty during the day, sometimes working them all at once in the many areas on the estate. He mainly uses albinos. To avoid confusion they are split into groups which live together and are marked with an animal friendly livestock marker, just like the ones used on sheep and pigs. Many use different coloured tape on their collars so if working similar ferrets you can notice at a glance which one keeps appearing and which one may have to be dug out.

The colour of the ferret (as discussed earlier) has no difference physically but mentally the colour can play a big role. The colour can make a big difference whilst working. Some prefer the white of the albino, some the dark polecat and all the varied colours in-between.

The albino, because it is white, stands out in thick dense undergrowth and grassland, but not in deep frost or a layering of snow. Some areas of Great Britain get more of the white stuff than others so some prefer the dark polecat colouring. Remember the only difference between all of these colours is just that, a different hair colour, but albinos are seen more easily in dense bushes and grass.

The age at which the ferret is worked varies dramatically. I tend to compare the entering of ferrets to that of entering a dog. You must make sure that the animal is mature enough, trained enough and started slowly. I train my ferrets from an early age by placing a lot of pipes, branches and layered shelving inside their court and this encourages them to not only to go down narrow tunnels but also to climb and explore different levels. As for net training and getting used to having a collar put on, or for the novice practising putting a collar on, I use the dummy warren I use for my show demonstrations. It has a small tunnel and a net placed over the end. This gets the ferret used to nets, especially with a collar on. But for those who haven't such a luxury you can recreate this by having a piece of drainage pipe and cut a plywood shape to stick the net onto and hey presto, a cheap simple training aid.

If the ferret is the young of the summer wait until the turn of winter, about October/November time. The ferrets will be about seven or eight months old and used to being handled in all situations they should be ready to start, but there are always exceptions. These might take a little longer but remember you have a few years of work ahead of you; an extra month or two isn't going to hurt is it?

Start them in a simple warren, preferably behind an experienced ferret, but normally many are starting with a couple of novice ferrets so make it as much fun as possible for these youngsters. A nice four-hole warren with a gradual sloping entrance hole is ideal. Don't try to force the ferret down a steep hole or any other, just let nature take its course. If you force a ferret down or go to snatch it from the hole you might encourage it to skulk or refuse to enter and play about at the entrance to the warren. Skulking is when the ferret comes to the surface of the hole but keeps just out of hands' reach. This can be overcome with time and encouragement, but prevention is better than a cure. As for ferrets refusing to enter a particular hole, their nose is far better than ours, what if something has already been there, like a stoat for example? Yes, a stoat will bolt away from a ferret but the rabbits will have gone as well. Never force your ferret to go underground.

The ferrets need to learn at their pace, not ours.

The jill is the more commonly used ferret, as it is smaller and keener to work but tires quicker. The hob is larger, starts and finishes at the same pace but with the sizes increasing the hobs are able to grab, kill and drag around the rabbit underground making marking a harder job than it should be. But the choice is entirely yours.

Whatever sex or colour you choose or indeed have, please remember that the ferrets are not designed to be chucked at a hole or bank, you must place them as close as is possible, even lifting the net to allow them in. It's not the end of the world to carry out such a simple task is it?

Ferret carrying boxes
The ferrets will then need something to be transported about in. The main points to consider in transporting your ferrets are reliability, practicality and security.

When the ferret is spoken about or seen, the first image is that of sticking them down one's trousers. You may laugh but this was one of many madcap methods of transporting the ferret. When ferreting was confined to the noble few the poacher had to carry his animals around without them being noticed. A small pocket was sewn into the trouser waist and the ferret was then placed inside this. After all they weren't going to walk around with it in a large box for all to see were they?

This method was for the brave, let's stick with the more conventional means. But what is conventional?

The earliest of ferreters first used sacks for transportation, but what about the poor ferret? Sacks were not only cold but offered the ferret no comfort and also no protection either from clumsy oafs like me and my size nines! A better way had to be found. Boxes of all shapes and sizes were used, wicker, wood, metal and lately plastic. Because of the nature of the ferret, security was the main concern as these animals are the Houdinis of the animal world.

Some of these weren't ideally suited for the needs of the ferret as in the case of the metal cases. Metal heats up in the summer causing the inside to sweat but more alarming is the impact in winter. The metal freezes in the winter months causing all sorts of unthinkable injuries connected with freezing metal and the ferret's skin.

So a more manageable material needs to be used – wood. This is more manageable and opens the door for all different designs. Many boxes through time were tried and tested, the more practical ones being copied throughout the country.

Many different designs and sizes of boxes

All the boxes above have one thing in common, they are all bowback ferret boxes, and a bowback sits nicely against the coat or body to ensure a silent and still journey for both ferret and ferreter. There is nothing worse than a box banging to and fro when carrying a lot of gear and rabbits, but you can use boxes with flat backs, it's up to you. Another advantage is that with the box tight and still you can shoot and work your dogs and ferrets with the box still attached to your back.

The ideal size of a box is 18 inches long by 9 inches high and 10 inches deep, with a wide comfortable strap, ample ventilation holes, a good hasp and staple catch with a clip that isn't hard to close, but hard enough to make sure you notice that it has been properly closed and so prevent any unauthorised leave. This ensures the box can be carried safely for both ferrets and ferreter. Some prefer a double compartment for a ferret each side, some prefer just a small single or a large single compartment box, again it's what suits you best that counts.

Wire cages and cat carriers can be, and indeed are, used in warm weather for travel but offer little or no practical protection in the ferreting months of the year.

Electronic ferret finders

One of the many improvements in the world of the ferret, especially the working ferret, has been the ferret finder, something which I hope all you ferreters use. Some panic when first starting to ferret and clamber across the warren after a couple of minutes. Chill – let the ferret do its work before getting the receiver out.

Before this modern technology was designed, there was several ways of ferret retrieval. The majority of ferrets were either coped/muzzled to prevent killing or had teeth broken or sawn off – all acts of gross cruelty on behalf of the ferret. In the early days the ferreter worked the jills loose. The hob had a different role when the jill worked (lying up) below ground; the hob was wearing a collar and attached to this was 25-yard line, knotted at 1-yard intervals. The jill then surfaced and was boxed up. The ferreter then followed the line dug up and retrieved the ferret and rabbit. Just imagine what these ferreters had to go through. Just imagine how many digs were required to find the ferret and many call this trenching.

Many still advocate this method, some even swear by it. I suppose it's the age we live in. But why dig three or four holes instead of just one? This method mustn't be forgotten though as it could come in useful if, when you are out, anything happens to your ferret finder set which consists of a receiver set and a collar to which you can then add as many collars as you wish.

The collar comes in two depths, eight and fifteen feet depths, the eight foot also comes in a micro set which is about half the size of the conventional one. The transmitter is carried on a leather collar; this fits around the ferret's neck. *See picture.*

Because of the substances encountered underground it is advisable to cover the transmitter on the collar with water-proof electrician's tape, this will not only keep it safe and dry but will prevent the screw top from working loose, especially as the rabbit is prone to dish out hefty kicks to the ferret. It is also handy to put a brightly coloured tape around the receiver or in my case I paint them bright orange. *See picture.*

If only I had a pound for every time they have been put down and temporarily lost because of the drab grey colouring.

When the ferret is working there are several reasons why it may refuse to return to the surface. It may have forced a rabbit into a 'stop' and is refusing to leave the rabbit. It could have killed a rabbit below or, as I will explain, the ferret could be trapped in one of the many passages inside the warren.

Whilst ferreting can bring many problems, the problem of trapping can be a potentially lethal one. This is where the transmitter comes into its own.

The warren was designed for the rabbit, by the rabbit, and they are considerably larger than the ferret. Therefore the width of the burrows is as large as the rabbit. The ferret can sometimes find this to be a difficulty when working. One of the designs of the warren is a 'stop' and these can point in all directions. These are the rabbit's safe spots. Because the rabbit has very little nerves in the rear quarters it can feel no pain. This is used as a defence mechanism when threatened. The rabbit squeezes into the stop head first with its rear protecting it. When these passages are upwards or drop to another stop the rabbit uses its body to grip the sides thus enabling it to climb a sheer vertical drop or climb. But unfortunately as the ferret is smaller it cannot copy this move, or when using two or more ferrets it is not uncommon for one ferret to drive the rabbit towards the other ferret, which in turn kills the rabbit and then traps itself in the progress. The ferret is now trapped, unable to climb. With the invention of the locator this is a problem easily overcome.

Whilst digging to your ferret care should be taken. The spade of an over active digger often injures ferrets. Not only is there the danger of decapitation but also of the loose soil falling in and suffocating the animal.

The probe is used to check the depth of the void of the burrow from the surface where you are digging. This tool is invaluable when dealing with these vertical drops.

When the dig has to start remember to start the hole at the centre of the reading and work around this reading. If turf has to be removed place it upside-down and put all of the removed earth on top of it. Because some ferrets move when the thuds of the spade are heard check the locator every now and then to make sure it is still there.

When you have reached to within a foot of the reading test the direction with the probe. This will enable you to break through to the exact spot of the burrow. When you have broken through be extra careful not to cave in the hole. As with a lot of things in ferreting, experience is the best source of knowledge. After a few digs you will know what to do and be able to perfect your digging skills.

Nets

Rabbits by nature are quite unpredictable at times; the same can be said for a day spent in the company of your ferrets and dog and if there is one thing that I have learnt is that you can take nothing for granted where nature is concerned.

When it comes to setting nets you must take into account the rabbit's means of exiting its warren. Many people give a false impression that every rabbit bolts out of the ground at 100 mph, they don't. The rabbit, if in dense woodland or ditches filled with undergrowth, may creep away and try to escape by creeping along a ditch bottom or through some thick hedging, cover which they feel safe in. When they creep out your net must be set correctly and not obstructed by any twigs or brambles or the rabbit will simply hit the net and without closing it and will retreat. This is when you must decide on which nets to use.

Nets are made in many materials – hemp, nylon or there are many of the different grades of knotless nets which are made from a type of synthetic cord and these are becoming quite popular as they are heavier than nylon but without the after care of hemp. You can get both good and bad nets from any material but I would suggest a good quality hemp net as opposed to the cheaper nylon nets. Hemp is a natural material so it requires more attention after a day's ferreting but the ease in handling is far better than nylon. Some tend to find nylon light and difficult to work either in windy or woodland situations as they are very light and attract every twig in the neighbourhood, and they tend to slip, this then hinders the slick pursing action of the net and allows the rabbit to escape. If you do go for nylon, go for a heavy duty net. Hemp holds the rabbits better without the net slipping and enabling the rabbit to kick itself free.

You can use purse nets, long nets to surround an area or whole hedge, or a combination of both.

For those starting out, pick a small warren; it will be easier to net and for you to keep an eye on without panicking. If you do not have enough nets, pick the best holes and fill the rest in, this way you may get more digs but the dig will be literally inches from the surface. Net all you can, check for the little boltholes especially those vertical shafts that are often covered in grass and you don't realise are there until you are staring at the rabbit's backside running in the opposite direction.

It may be advisable to keep one or two nets spare so when your first rabbit hits the net you can dispatch it in the net, replace the net with another one straight away and then remove the rabbit from the first net. After time you will get the knack of this but sometimes one or two hit the net at the same time and this method comes in useful. Many place their size nines down the hole to prevent the rabbit from running out whilst dealing with the rabbit and then replacing the net straight away. It's up to you but remember that your body only has two feet and if more than one rabbit hit the nets at the same time you may curse yourself for not getting into the habit of dispatching in the net and replacing it straight away and then go back to the netted rabbit – it is dead, it isn't going anywhere.

You want to ensure that NO nets are left behind; there are a number of ways you can help your memory. Count and pack nets in bundles of 10, fasten each net with an elastic band. When using a net put the band around your wrist, if any bands are left there must be a net somewhere. Or make a mental note of how many nets you have and where, and stick to it. Usually with a bit of practice you will remember where the nets are, especially if you have painted the peg tops bright orange as they will stick out.

Long nets
A long net is exactly what the name implies, a long net ranging from 5, 10, 25 yards to over 100 yards in length. These nets usually have two yards of bagging for every yard in length to ensure the rabbits are caught and do not bounce off. Although difficult and time consuming to learn how to use, once mastered they are invaluable when ferreting large warrens or ferreting alone or with a dog.

The nets are run out with an end pin or crook on each end of the top and bottom cords to give stability and tension when putting the pegs in. These pegs are usually made from hazel or privet but lately glass fibre pegs have been used. These pegs fasten to both top and bottom lines about every seven or so paces.

Long nets are used to great effect as stop nets. Place them in between the rabbits' warren and their avenue of escape, or surrounding a warren completely so nothing can escape. This usually ensures you avoid a lengthy spell laying a lot of purse nets.

When using these nets with a dog get it used to the net as many simply chase a rabbit into the net and become entangled themselves setting the rabbit free in the process.

Practice putting these nets down and picking them up again before attempting to use them for ferreting otherwise you will spend your day untangling the nets. You can get these nets already made up with the pegs attached to the net so it is easier to use. This method is used for small 5- or 10-yard nets that are used to cross hedges and ditches with ease or 50 yards plus for surrounding whole warrens.

Setting a long net

Rabbit caught in long net

Rabbits at home.
Dog marking inhabited warren, ready for the ferret to bolt the rabbit.

Ferreting dogs
Many a countryman has a dog as a companion and the same goes for the ferreter. Many different types can be used – lurchers, terriers or gun dogs if the rabbits are to be shot but as with shooting there is no place for an unruly or disobedient dog in the field.

Many good books and videos have been produced concerning the use of dogs alongside the ferrets and humans as a rabbiting team par excellence.

A successful retrieve.

In my mind the ideal ferreting dog has to be very obedient, biddable, broken to all stock especially game birds, have a good coat and be small and brave enough to enter bushes after those rabbits that refuse to break cover. But more importantly I don't want a fast dog, no, I want a quick dog, a thirty yarder, quick enough to catch the rabbit on the run before it reaches safety but canny enough to find and surprise those sitting rough when out walking an area in. A dog that marks an inhabited warren will not only save you hours of time but will add a substantial amount of rabbits to your tally over the years.

But am I asking too much? After all, the dog I have described is probably the direct opposite to my bitch, Bramble. But as I have watched all my dogs grow so has my knowledge and experience in training them. That is one of the merits of working your own dog, training it and watching it make mistakes and the joy she gives you as you watch her correct them and the reward she brings you back.

But lately it pains me to watch her chase the escapees from our ferreting forays knowing that her time is coming to an end as at the time of writing she is now nearly ten years old.

I just wish the men in grey suits in the capital could just grasp how much more there is to working dogs than just fox hunting. For me there are no greater companions than my lurcher and spaniel, after all they don't answer me back, although their expressions are far worse to live with sometimes!

I was going to ask for advice, but to be honest I have had a tremendous amount of advice and this has just added to my confusion and given me a headache.

You see the problem is that humans, especially from region to region, live in totally different landscapes and many have not experienced ferreting in different areas and the different problems they bring. The rabbit catchers of the area have their choice of dog and of course they have worked well for them. But I could stick half a dozen very good dogs and ferret men and women in a room and I could bet money on the outcome. Utter chaos.

Some ferreters swear by the terrier because they are small, agile and have a nose that many cannot argue with. The coat on a good terrier will withstand the bushes and the barbed wire in pursuit of rabbits. I have a particular liking for terriers, especially crossed with a whippet, as they have a spirit about them though many have a down side. Some people say that a terrier will only do what a terrier wants or feels like, but many have not been trained like you would your lurcher so you can't blame the dog. I like, as many, to have a silent dog when out ferreting and unfortunately in my experience terriers are far from silent.

In recent times I have read about, but unfortunately not seen, the sporting Lucas terrier or one of Brian Plummer's terriers. Now apparently these are a credit to the terrier world, they hunt and retrieve but are they the ideal ferreting dog as they lack the pace to catch the fleeing coney?

I have purposely kept the section on terriers short, but lurchers, well, where do I start?

They is nothing more pleasing to the eye than a well-trained dog and nothing turns my stomach more than an untrained dog out ferreting. Sadly more and more have entered the ferreting world with little training and the ferret is the loser in that particular argument.

The collie cross, favoured by many to the terrier crosses, and the vast amount of different crosses from Australian cattle dogs to the reverse bred dogs like the reverse three-quarter collie whippet, a scruffy little dog but I have seen many good ferreting dogs of this mix. The problem is I keep getting the same advice be it up north or down south. Advice from the collie cross owner
is keep with the collie and don't touch the terrier crosses, the advice from the terrier cross is vice versa, so who do I listen to? After all you want to make the right choice. It just goes to show just how friendly country sport-orientated people are, but for once this is causing me a headache.

I remember an old rabbit catcher from the Black Country telling me to ignore all advice and go from the heart. Make a mental picture of what you want from a dog and how you want it to look and perform, and go for it. Perhaps he was right! But that is little consolation in the search for that dog I described earlier on.

If I was looking for a ferreting dog that I can introduce to my team (we may not be the most prolific rabbit catchers like those on Salisbury Plain or the rabbit infested countryside of say Hampshire, but what we do I am are happy with and more importantly so are the landowners) if I was looking for a replacement I could introduce to my team, I would go for a bitch with a good coat and be up to 20" at the shoulder, quick but biddable. This was my vision of the perfect dog for me, so all those who I am going to disappoint, sorry, but at the end of the day it is me who will train her, so any shortcoming will be down to me.

On my travels I see a lot of first cross terrier-whippet/greyhounds, but then again I have seen some very good collie crosses and I liked what I saw. Not everybody's cup of tea, but that is what makes us human and not sheep.

Whatever dog you have or are thinking of having I would strongly recommend reading one of the many top quality lurcher-training books. But remember, a good dog will add to your arsenal and a bad dog, an unruly dog, will add not only to your distractions but will be more likely to get you into trouble with the land-owner/farmer and make it more difficult to keep your permission, so take care.

Knives
No countryman/woman should ever leave home without a knife. With the rise in popularity of the multi-functional knives, more people are using these today, but many still use the traditional lock or sheath knife. Whatever knife is used makes sure it is sharp. A blunt knife is only good for stirring your tea with!

Probe
This is a long metal T bar used for probing the soil to find the exact position of the burrow. Some have a bulge about four inches from the tip. This will move freely when the probe has broken through to the burrow, I feel that you only need a straight T bar like the one shown with the rest of the equipment. A lot of people don't use these but I find them invaluable, especially for beginners as they may get carried away with the spade and cause a nasty accident to their prized ferrets.

Mobile phone
Ferreting is done in places away from anyone, in weather that sends most to the fireplace and often alone. So what would you do if you or one of your animals had an accident and needed help fast? You would be surprised how easy it is for a dig to cave in, to stick a leg in a hole and break it or simply twist an ankle so you are unable to walk for help.

Always ensure you have a phone and that you can get coverage with it and tell somebody who and where you are and when you expect to return, especially as the time of year ferreting takes place, if the weather changes suddenly in certain areas like the moors or marshes, you could be in serious trouble and need help. Remember – better to be safe than sorry.

Ferret trap-box
This is a box that has been designed around a conventional cage trap, but with solid sides. This I have seen used to marvellous effect by the warreners on my travels. It may be handy to keep one or two just in case.

Spade
Sometimes called a graft, the spade plays a bigger part in ferreting than most people realise. As it is the tool that will be used to retrieve your ferrets, you will have to make sure it is the right one as tradition alone does not dig the hole for you!

In the small areas of Suffolk and Norfolk I ferret, you would be amazed at the different soil structures encountered – sandy dunes, fine soil by the coast through to the clays of the East Anglian farms. That it is why the choice of spade or spades is vital. It must be hard wearing and sharp edged, but more importantly comfortable to the user. The spade must be able to dig efficiently into whatever soil is present, including the depth. Remember that could be up to and beyond 8 feet in depth.
Pictures and stories of people using long-handled grafts are ideal, if they are practicable. Because of the varied soils I use an angled head and handle spade (see photograph of ferreting equipment to see selection of different spades used) these enable me to dig any type of soil I may encounter and any depth to be dug out successfully.

Note: Explore what soil you have and find a reliable, comfortable spade, what may suit me and our Suffolk soil may not suit you and your Yorkshire ground.

That little piece of extra equipment you may choose to carry
These are non-essentials that are always needed when you don't have them! Some of these items might seem a bit ridiculous but let me assure you, they work. These separate the beginner from the professional in many ways. When dealing with a rabbit problem you may have to prune back bushes, clear a path for your long nets or dig through stones to reach your ferrets.
I have outlined the essential tools for a day's ferreting. An assortment of ground

clearance tools, which range from a scythe, billhook and pocket saw to clear roots when digging to secateurs. These are handy when you have to do some drastic clearance. Constant kneeling in the wet and cold conditions can play havoc with your knees. Gardener's or builder's knee pads can not only save you from grief now but in many years time. The same could be said for thick gardening gloves as well, but only for clearance work.

Encountering clay and ballast whilst digging is a frustrating experience but what can you use to speed up the retrieval of both ferret and hopefully rabbit? Across the country you can find army surplus stores and these are Aladdin's caves for many a sports person. After several struggles with compact clay I used a mini pick-axe/shovel and this is always kept in the car now after saving the day many times.

One item that should be carried by all, but sadly isn't, is a first aid kit – probably the most underrated piece of equipment, often forgotten about until it is needed. Because of the nature of ferreting in wild and often remote locations and the equipment used a first aid kit is often needed. It is not only for your animals but also for you and your friends as well. This is another reason to repeat that you should never leave without your mobile phone, especially if ferreting alone or/ and in remote places, especially in winter when the weather can change in a flash.

Clothing
Clothing to the ferreter plays a major part in the health and well being of, yes, the ferreter. Firstly it keeps you warm, comfortable and dry and hopefully not making you stick out like a sore thumb. By this I mean not wearing brightly coloured garments, however warm they may be. Although the rabbit is colour blind, in its world of grey a bright colour will show up. This will not only alarm it into not bolting but any rabbits sitting rough will head in the opposite direction. The drab colouring blend into the surroundings and also attract unwanted attention to you.
Because of the time of the year you will be spending at the beck and call of nature there are vital areas of your body to keep warm and dry. Keep these happy and the rest of your body will feel the benefits. Usually ferreting clothes are old and therefore you're not too fussed if they get torn and dirty. A pocket torch will come in handy if you do any ferreting in thick hedges. When having to dig in thick, wide hedging you may be glad of the extra light when looking at what you are digging and once you have broken through to the chamber. Let us take a closer look at your feet, body and head.

Footwear

During the time you spend walking, digging and standing about, if you wear in-adequate footwear your feet will suffer and this will spread upwards, and believe me there is nothing worse than ferreting, and especially digging, with cold feet. Make sure your choice is the right one; after all they're your feet. Be it a good stout pair of work or walking boots or Wellingtons make sure they are man enough for the job ahead. Ferreting inevitably means digging and any footwear must be up to and be comfortable to dig in. Check any potential Wellington boots soles as many will cripple your feet when digging properly with your feet and not just throwing the spade into the ground with your arms as many do!

Hats or caps

They say that the greatest loss of heat is through your head – keep this warm and dry and the rest of your body follows. Hats vary, some simple, some extreme, again make sure they do the job. Spectacle wearers have an extra burden with rain so a peaked cap or bushman's hat is the order of the day. From woolly hats to the bushman's all have their ups and downs. Get what suits you, whatever it may look like to an outsider.

Jackets

As rabbiting is mainly carried out in the harshest time of year, usually between August and March, a good jacket is required. The weather tries its hardest to ensure that you are giving a second glance at the conditions and not what you are doing – ferreting that warren. Snow, rain and howling winds combine to give that little distraction which, with sod's law, makes the difference between a rabbit in the bag or it running away into the next county. That is why, when talking about ferreting equipment, it is just as important to mention clothing and jackets in particular as it is nets or ferret finders.

The development of materials used for the making of jackets over the last decade or so has been amazing, the likes of Gore-Tex and tweeds now rubbing shoulders with the good old wax jacket in the field as well as for normal use. But buyer be-ware, you will require a special jacket for ferreting, one that will put up with bushes, trees and the like, so the material has to be rugged and consistent. Ferret-ing can and will test any jacket. As I dive into a bush, when I reappear I expect to still be wearing a jacket, not leaving half of it behind in the bush.

Our dear old friend Mr Rabbit isn't stupid; the entrances to his home are usually in the most inhospitable places around, where he feels a strong sense of security.

In my experience this rules out ordinary Gore-Tex, but some of the latest jackets have Gore-Tex lining as in the army ones and these do last a little longer. Tweed jackets have recently reduced in price so a great many are used and although warm they collect water and mud and have a tendency to attract every piece of thorn to them just for you to find when least expecting it. My own personal favourite is the wax jacket as when ferreting we need something strong and sturdy with good zips and plenty of pockets.

But don't just stick to one. I have many – from the Barbour jacket to an old Belgium army jacket with a Gore-Tex lining that is an excellent ferreting jacket. But at the end of the day the choice is yours. Whatever jacket you wear ensure that underneath, if you want to keep warm, wear plenty of layers of clothing as these layers will trap the heat and prevent unwanted heat release throughout the day's ferreting.

Over-trousers
Wax over-trousers should also be a part of the kit. Some use chaps but these have no protection for your bottom, so remember this before sitting down on the grass! In recent years many, including myself, have started to use old army Gore-Tex over-trousers, but only in open spaces such as grazing or heath land where we are not in or near bushes as they have a tendency to tear. In these places I use my old wax over trousers, that way when I sit down to have cup of tea I stay dry!

Some wear gloves when ferreting but this can cause all sorts of problems when handling ferrets that aren't used to them, as well as snagging on bushes. The choice is yours.

Remember that not only must you take care of your ferreting equipment but also your personal equipment as well if don't want it to let you down, by then it will be too late, you'll be wet and cold – urghhh!

Ready for any weather

Yourself and your stomach
Prepare a flask with a hot drink inside, a few biscuits etc. for the day ahead and a little drink for your ferrets and dog – you never know just what the day ahead holds in store for you and your dog and ferrets.

Be confident when preparing to go ferreting, if you are unsure and begin to doubt anything you won't enjoy the day as you should, and that would be a crime in itself.

One step further – making your own nets

These instructions are a guide – there are net making videos available as there are net making kits. I would strongly advise anyone to take the time and patience and learn to make your own nets. Not only is it a fraction of the cost and you can tailor-make your nets to suit your needs but also the satisfaction of catching consistently in nets you have made yourself is an indescribable feeling.

Follow these instructions and illustrations and this will be a good start to your net-making future. These are just basic instructions and not a strict guideline, many prefer to do things slightly differently but this is the way I learnt. I know many who begin by starting straight off the ring but I would recommend learning how to knit your basic net before expanding to such an exercise. The net making videos deal with this in greater detail.

Equipment needed: needle, hemp, mesh gauge, drawcord, 1" rings (2 per net), scissors/knife and patience. *See picture.*

First fill the needle. Hold the needle in the left hand, point upwards towards the ceiling. Place the free end of the hemp on one side, under the thumb (Fig 1) then around the tongue, down the same side (over the free end) and around the bottom. Now, turn the needle round and lead the twine up the other side, around the tongue and down again. Turn the needle and continue until the needle is filled. Cut off the twine leaving a tail. The twine should be kept taught and pulled firmly into position during filling the needle.

The beginners guide to making a purse net

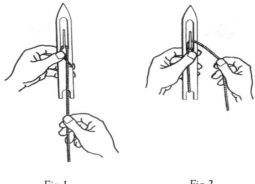

Fig 1   *Fig 2*

To 'set-up' the net, a short piece of twine (the base line) is tied between two hooks. Once mastered many will wish to either put the first row directly onto the 1" ring which will be held onto a hook by a length of twine or a hook. But first learn to walk! On this base line a row of fifteen loops or half meshes is made by forming a series of clove hitches along it working from left to right. (Once mastered the net maker will do it whichever way they prefer.) This is done by leaving 3 feet of spare twine and proceeding as shown in Figs 3 and 4, or 3 and 5, depending on whether you prefer fingers or the mesh gauge provided. After the first row a guide MUST be used in order to keep the meshes of uniform size; this is vital if your net is to work.

The second row is now started, working from left to right. The knots from now on are to be sheep bends formed on the ends of the loops (half meshes) you have already completed. Holding the gauge in the left hand, a little way below the 15th loop (the last mesh of the setting up row) bring the needle down in front of it, up behind it and then through the loop from the far side towards you – Fig 6. Now pull the needle strongly towards you until the upper edge of the gauge is brought hard up against the tip of the 15th loop. Grip the loop and twine at this point and hold it tightly against the top of the gauge – Fig 7. Now with a clockwise swing of the right hand (indicated by the arrow) cause the twine between the left hand and the needle to form a loop. Then pass the needle behind both bars of half mesh 15 and out through the loop formed – Fig 8. Pull tight and a sheet bend is formed – Fig 9. Having made this first mesh, others of the second row are formed one after another in the same way until the end of the row, all newly formed meshes are lying side by side around your gauge, with a neat line of knots at the top of the gauge. You only completely remove the gauge when you reach the end of each row of new meshes you have just formed. At this point the work can be turned on its base line so that the 3rd row can be a repeat of the 2nd. If you turn the work on the completion of each new row, you will continue to work left to right. Each additional row adds a further 2 inches to your net. Therefore, using the gauge, a 3-foot rabbit purse net will require 18 rows of netting.

To complete the net you will have to refill the needle more than once, to do this simply tie on where you ran out of twine but try to make the joining knot appear halfway down the mesh so it doesn't interfere with your knots at the top or bottom of the mesh. Having hopefully completed your first sheet of netting measuring 18 rows by 15 rows, cut off the twine from the needle leaving about a yard (3 feet) of twine hanging to your net.

With your fingers and guide, make a final row of meshes on the 1 inch end ring, using only your fingers to do so. Finish the row and tie off at the knot a couple of meshes up (4 inches) on the end of the net.

Remove the base line at the top of your net, turn your netting so that the fitted ring is at the top and suspend it from this ring, on a hook or similar fixing. Using the spare end of twine you left free when you started, braid the second 1-inch ring onto what was originally the top end of your netting. You have now a sheet of hemp netting with a top and bottom ring. To finish this off you will require a draw cord and peg. To do this you can reeve your braided drawcord through the bottom ring, back down through your meshes on the other side and through the first ring again.

Stretch the netting to its full length and leave around 12 inches of your drawcord hanging at the bottom of your net and cut it off at this point. Add to this cord your net peg. Your net peg wants to be sturdy to last; the head wants to be large enough to prevent it from coming through the top and bottom ring (*see picture Page 80*), tie peg to draw cord and you have just completed your first rabbit purse net.

Earlier on you will have read about a net called a poke net. To make these all you need to do is make the net slightly longer, 4 or 5 feet long and instead of having one peg these have two, one at each end. (*See picture Page 80*).

Whatever size you want or need your nets to be the process is the same, just add on to the length with extra meshes.

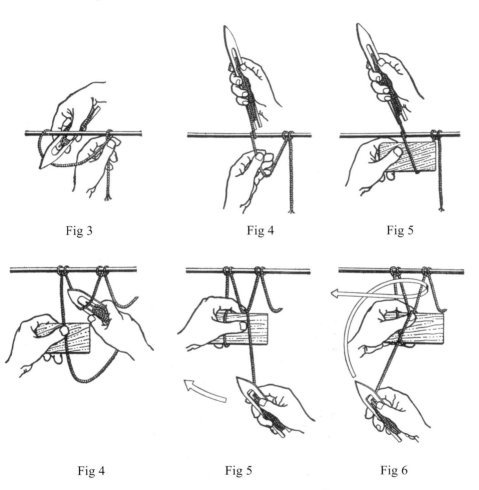

Fig 3   Fig 4   Fig 5

Fig 4   Fig 5   Fig 6

Fig 9

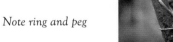

Purse net peg: note how its end is too large to fall through the peg and its orange tip which helps you spot the peg thus avoiding a lost net. Orange is a better colour than white or yellow as these tend to merge with frost or snow.

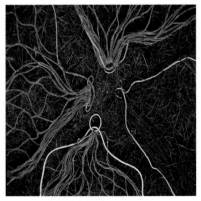

Hemp, nylon and knotless nets with runners and rings

Chapter 5

Preparation, preparation, preparation

Getting you and your equipment to know each other before your day's ferreting

Preparation is the key word before embarking on any day's ferreting. It is no good looking the part if you cannot use competently your equipment. After all, the future of your ferret may be at stake. Time taken training with your ferrets and equipment is time well spent. What is the use of having a ferret finder set if you don't know how to use it properly, have nice new set of nets but don't know how to lay them properly? Just because you have a load of gadgets it doesn't necessarily mean that you are a better ferreter or will catch more rabbits. Many I know use the barest of equipment and consistently obtain good results.

But even if you are not a beginner, take time to look at and test your kit well before your first outing of the new season to ensure the gremlins or mice haven't checked out it first. A friend of mine, known as Dave the Fox, promised me a couple of longnets he had in his shed. Imagine his surprise when he took them out at the last minute just to find that the local mouse population had shredded them all for bedding along with his fishing seat and tackle. We didn't take the mick, well not much anyway.

But it just goes to show that everything needs to be checked and if anything is amiss you have time to order some new gear to go ferreting – don't leave it until the night before. And that includes your clothing as well.

Let's start with the ferret first. There are a number of jobs it needs to learn before you take it out ferreting. It must be used to being handled in any situation without reacting with its teeth. You must get it used to wearing a collar with the transmitter attached, be used to its carrying box and last but not least, get it used to passing through nets, especially with a collar on.

I have taken it for granted that your ferret is well used to being handled and this will be invaluable when getting it used to wearing the transmitter collar or, if you are to use a dog, to get your ferret and dog to know each other.

As discussed earlier, the size of hobs are growing larger and one piece of advice when working hobs, especially big hobs, (the size is now such that these extremely powerful ferrets can not only easily kill a rabbit but also drag one around the warren) is that getting an easy accurate mark may be difficult. Understand your ferrets and their capabilities; don't get too downhearted if this happens to you, it happens to us all. That is why the majority use jills as they are smaller, quicker and generally have a better attitude for work. But not all ferrets are the same shape and size so you may have some small hobs and large jills!

Ensure the collar is tight but not too tight. If needed add one or two extra holes with a nail (preferably when not on the ferret's neck!) One way to check if it's ok is to pull the collar forward and it shouldn't go over the skull. Twist the collar around the neck gently without tearing great lumps of fur out, and if neatly rotated 360 degrees then it is not strangling your ferret and therefore not getting it into bad habits or being afraid of collars. You may need some assistance when first starting to put these collars on but with a little practice you should be doing it with out any help.

Getting the ferret used to the travelling box should have started when it first arrived and every time its hutch is cleaned. It may scratch at the sides and top but this is normal, nothing to worry about, although irritating. You may just want to place your box away from any areas worked to avoid unnecessary noise or irritation. But the main reason is that inside the box you probably have a ferret with another transmitter collar on and this will give you a false mark when trying to find the ferret in the warren. It also goes without saying that any collars you may have in your pockets ensure that they are not active and sending out a signal. You would be surprised just how often I hear of this problem.

One practice many fail to do is getting the ferrets used to passing through nets. This takes time to learn but with a little practice and patience at home with some drainpipe and a nice net, once in the field it won't make such a mess of every net it encounters. Although many say that a ferret cannot pass through a net with a collar on this appears to be an easy excuse for not using one.

So there we have it – a ferret used to hands, collars, nets and its carrying box. Now to use the ferret finder sets, and properly. Once bought, read the instructions on how to use, don't leave it until it's too late, but just in case I will run through it anyway.

The ferret finder set has revolutionised ferreting. The options before were limited and back breaking, many still use these methods but why not use technology if it saves time, gets extra rabbits and saves the lives of many ferrets from getting needlessly lost or abandoned, especially when they could only be six inches away from you?

It is my opinion that no one should work a ferret without one of these sets, unless competent in using a liner or a liner without the pull cord and replaced with a transmitter collar. But even still, why dig half a dozen holes when one will suffice? But the final decision is up to you, I can only offer my advice.

Get you ferret finder set and put a new 9v PP3 battery in the receiver, ensuring it is correctly connected. I would strongly advise you not use re-chargeable batteries as these will give a false depth mark because they have a different strength than normal batteries.

Place a new battery in the collar being careful not to over tighten the cap as this will puncture the battery and therefore shorten its working life. Again, if you use a hearing aid battery, which is a zinc-air battery, these are only 1.4 volts and rely on air for their reliability when in use, so not only is the battery weaker the signal strength is weaker too and so the marks are unreliable. But the zinc air batteries require air circulation to work reliably, something which, once fitted and covered by electricians tape and put six feet under the ground, may be fine in a hearing aid, and they do work but what we want is consistency. Use the proper 1.55 volt high drain silver oxide batteries recommended by the manufacturer, Deben Group Industries.

Make sure before fitting the battery that the rivet and inside of the battery cap are clean to ensure a proper connection for the battery. Tighten the cap so it is finger tight, and not rock solid tight as this will puncture the battery and you will have erratic readings all day long.

Cover the collar with electrician's tape before a day's ferreting – not only does this stop mud, dirt and water from trying to interfere with its workings but it offers protection from kicks that the rabbit may delve out in the warrens underground.

After all it is you what will be digging all those extra holes, think of your back and bag.

Ferret finder set
8 foot, 8 foot micro and 15 foot collars
Cap off, battery fitted and taped up awaiting fitting to ferret

You now have a ferret finder set consisting of your receiver and collar, or collars. Whatever depth set you have place the collar on the floor so it appears as it would when on the ferret, with the transmitter flat on the floor as it would be under the ferret's chin when in use. If you want you could do this on some grass so you cannot physically see the collar, but to begin with we will do it in full view – better to be safe than sorry.

Switch your receiver on, turning your dial so it is at full depth, either 8 or 15 feet. The dial has these numbers on but the true reading is not the top end or bottom, but at the point in the middle of the dial, as this picture illustrates.

Note dial position

Keep the receiver at a constant height above the ground, do not follow the contours of the land but keep it level as this will avoid interference being picked up.

The receiver will emit a bleeping noise reminiscent of a Geiger counter. Move away from the collar left to right, slowly reducing the depth in feet on the dial. Once the clicking has stopped you have reached the point where you want to look at the dial and move a little closer until the clicking starts again. This is usually done in a criss-cross movement as you are trying to locate your collar in the centre of a large x shape. Keep doing this, reducing the depth until you have reached a point where you cannot reduce the depth any more or move away. (If the receiver makes an annoying constant burring sound reduce the depth completely or switch off and start again, it is just interference.) You now have a mark, a point that when you dig straight down, or in this case look directly down, you have your collar.

Practice makes perfect. Make a note of just how deep the collar is when the dial is virtually off, usually about six to ten inches, but this differs with different stages in the battery's life and the soil conditions.

You will encounter objects that may affect this process, electric fencing for one, and a lot of underground metal/metallic objects or low overhead electric cables. Where electric fencing is a problem ask if it can be switched off from time to time as all you will pick up are the clicks of the current passing through the fence. But these things are sent to try us, aren't they? .

Always, after every day out, remove the batteries from the finder set. Nothing is more annoying than false signals because of weak batteries.

One piece of advice that many will give you for sure is to paint your receiver box a bright colour like orange. These drab grey boxes are in the process of getting a revamp but until then you want to ensure yours isn't added to the list of many that have been buried and lost after a dig when filling the hole in. You will become accustomed to the use and benefits of this little gadget and will soon see what the benefits are of using one, but what it does give you is confidence knowing that you can track your ferrets if anything goes amiss.

If that's not for you the other option is the old traditional liner. Although outdated it is useful to know how it works and have a collar and line in your kit bag just in case anything happens to your ferret finder set.

Before this modern technology was designed, there was several ways of ferret retrieval. The majority of ferrets were either coped/muzzled to prevent killing or had teeth broken or sawn off – all acts of gross cruelty on behalf of the ferret, something which I am glad to say hardly ever happens in this day and age. In the early days the ferreter worked the jills loose. The hob had a different role – one of confinement, loneliness and resentment. When the jill worked (lying up) below ground, the hob was wearing a collar. Attached to this was 25-yard line, knotted at 1-yard intervals. As the hob was subjected to loneliness he resented the jills. Jealousy made him think that what they had he wanted and he drove them off. When he was unleashed to find the jill and what she had, he found what he thought was his. The jill then surfaced and was boxed up. The ferreter then followed the line by sticking his arm down the hole in which the liner started with a stick, he then tapped the roof of the burrow and dug where his arm was, this was then repeated until the ferret and rabbit were retrieved.

Just imagine what these ferreters had to go through. Picture the scene. Ten yards of line has been used. The ferret had gone four yards forward, one sideways and four back. You would think the ferret is 30 feet from you but is actually only a couple of feet away. Just imagine how many digs were required to find the ferret.

Many still advocate this method, some even swear by it. I suppose it's the age we live in. But why dig four or five holes instead of just one, but saying that it is still a useful skill to learn in case of an emergency.

Digging to your ferrets

Digging and ferreting go hand in hand like bread and butter, don't let anyone tell you differently. That is why you will need to know how to dig properly. It is not as silly as it sounds.

When digging down to your ferrets, and you will, you want to do it as quickly as possible and hopefully just the once at a time. Deeper holes will require a larger start to the hole so you can reach to the ferret and rabbit. It is no good digging a nice hole if you cannot use it – all you will have to do is enlarge it.

When starting take into consideration the ground, if it is grassland take the turf you started with and lay it upside down so this is the last piece put back and makes a nice neat finish. Many don't bother to fill their holes in and this has cost many a ferreter his permission and reputation. Always fill in your holes to the best of your capabilities. You will not always fill it to the top as you have disturbed the void of the burrow so this has to be filled in costing you valuable earth in the process, that is why when you dig you are missing a few inches at the top.

To dig deep start with a nice big opening about twice the size of the hole you expect to finish with, with smaller digs of up to two feet, just a spade's width will usually be sufficient. Remember it's your back you will hurt if you do not dig safely or use an unsuitable spade, however fashionable it may appear to be, if you are like me and want to use as little energy in digging, use a garden spade, it has a larger head so therefore you can remove more earth with each spade load and therefore reaching the ferret quicker.

A lot of people don't use a probe but I think it is an invaluable piece of kit. Once you get to within six inches from your reading check with the probe. The reasons are simple – avoiding accidents – but also the tunnels are sometimes on top of each other, you break through and there is nothing there. But it may be a few inches to the side or directly beneath it, so you could just check with the probe – it doesn't take up much room in your kit bag.

When you are digging, or have dug a hole, or if you are digging another or choose to fill it in when you have finished, don't forget to put a net over the hole. Never leave it unprotected, as you can be sure that that would be the hole from which a rabbit appears, especially when you are about to break through to the chamber/passage, this final few inches before the chamber sometimes provides the distraction or spur the rabbit on to escape the attentions of the ferret.

The ferret will sometimes temporarily move away from the rabbit when the noise and vibrations inform it that someone is on its way down, so be warned.

Once you have reached your ferret it may be determined to hang on to its catch upon removal from the tunnel. There are a number of methods used to ensure it loses its grip, the most reliable and safest is to pick up both rabbit and ferret, apply pressure on the ferret's skull between the eyes, just a little way above the nose and it will start to let go of the rabbit. Always check for other rabbits once you have pulled one out for many times you will encounter more than one in the same stop. Look at the rabbit's position when you break through. If it is not tightly snug it may mean that there are one or two, maybe more, in front of it, so always check – you may be pleasantly surprised.

After you have finished digging and have collected your ferret and rabbit do not forget to fill all the holes back in. Treat your land like you would your own. Many also fill in all the holes they have just ferreted as a matter of course, this ensures that when you return you can not only tell if any have come back but you will have fewer holes to net. If ferreting banks or ditches it pays dividends if you have a dog as if any are missed or bolted free and make for these holes, with them being filled in it gives the dog or you with your gun time to catch/shoot them.

Setting your nets and picking them back up again
Nothing is more annoying than the sight of a rabbit escaping from a poorly set purse net, or any net come to think of it.

Setting your purse net is simplicity itself. You place your net over the hole in a manner that will ensnare the fleeing rabbit, be it at 100 mph or 1 mph, as they don't always bolt like a bat out of hell. Make sure that the holes are free from twigs and debris that may cause your net to snag and therefore not work properly.

Following the series of photos explaining the setting of nets you will see the logic behind this method.

First place the lower ring (the one opposite to the end with the peg) just inside the mouth of the entrance/exit hole; spread the net out so it just covers the outside areas of the hole – not the great clumps of earth. If the rabbit appears from its hole not through the earth surrounding it, you will need the spare netting for your slack.

Ensure that the net is bagged in the middle. What this means is that the net isn't taught but it has plenty of slack or give in it.

Stretch the drawline cord that is attached to the peg so it is at the end of its length. This will ensure the net will begin to purse or close the moment the rabbit begins to hit the net. A common mistake is to have too much slack in this line and the net has to travel a foot or two before pursing and a lot of rabbits are lost this way. Some peg before setting the net but you cannot gauge the length of the drawline accurately if you do this, always peg it in last.

Watch out for the bolt holes, the little often-overlooked escape routes that the rabbit makes from the inside to escape from the stoats, weasels and of course ferrets, often noticed when a rabbit appears out of nowhere and makes good its escape. These holes are often deceptively small but a fleeing rabbit somehow always manages to squeeze through. Every hole must either be netted or filled in to prevent unwanted escapees.

For those holes that are vertical, the same method applies but with bagging in the centre of the net set like a mushroom. The spare netting will catch the jumping rabbit thus avoiding escapees.

Once the time has come to pick up your nets at the end of the warren, do so with a bit of care and attention as well as speed. Nets that are picked up without checking and the odd clean are often time consuming in resetting later in the day.

When picking up your net, pick it up by the ring furthest away from the peg, grab the drawcord and pull the peg out of the ground. Pick any debris from the mesh, straighten by stretching the net out straight from ring to ring and proceed to fold in halves, first in half, then again and again, finishing with the drawcord being spun around the middle of the net to ensure the net stays together inside your bag. Simplicity itself but this is another exercise that will require some practice.

Setting a purse net

Picking up and folding a purse net

Always ensure that all of your nets have been picked up.

As with everything connected with ferreting, practice and let experience be your teacher. Be patient, use your eyes and ears and you will experience some fantastic sights and sounds when on your travels in pursuit of rabbits as no two days, situations or results are the same.

Get used to being in the right positions when ferrets are at work.
Whilst you have placed your ferrets inside the warren remember that you are to place them closely, if not under the net itself or inside the entrance to the warren, be careful not to chuck them from a height thus risking injury to the ferret. It is a vitally important that you place yourself in the correct position to tackle the nets once the rabbit has been pursed or your ferret moves to above ground and you want to catch them both quickly and quietly. If you are shooting, extra care must be taken, especially when you have more than one gun and a hedge in-between them. These rabbits are going to bolt – they have sensed the ferret or are forced to bolt by the ferrets.

Keep the noise down to a minimum but more importantly do not go crashing around the top of the warren whilst your ferrets are doing their business, it will only make the rabbits more determined to stay put. The best place to stand and wait is at the front or side of the warren but not too far way that you have to sprint and therefore sound like a herd of elephants, just a quick dash of a couple of yards is sufficient or in a position where you can see all of your nets or holes. Many would lead you to believe that you need to be far away from the action or the warren. You want to be quick on the mark, but as quiet as possible – try not to let any rabbits have the chance of escaping.

Do not stand directly in front of the entrance/exit holes as the rabbit will see you at the last minute and turn back. You can stand fairly close as long as you stay still and with wearing drab clothing you will blend in with the background. When you look at the majority of rabbits that bolt they pause for a millisecond before bolting, this is when they will turn back if you are in their face.

Dogs are a different kettle of fish. I give mine the freedom to go wherever she wants to go, or her nose tells her, as she knows what is going on and indeed what's coming out before I do and in all these years it hasn't showed any signs of putting the rabbits off from bolting.

Only the rabbit knows if it is going to bolt, sometimes you can make a lot of noise and they still bolt freely, other days you can be silent and they opt for facing the ferrets.

This is one of the traits of nature and ferreting, the unpredictability of the day ahead.

And lastly a few thoughts on the weather because our climate is unpredictable to say the least. Ferreting can be carried out in most weathers but extremely windy days, especially easterly winds, tend to produce fewer rabbits. Always check the forecast, you don't want to be stranded in the middle of nowhere with your ferret underground and in the middle of a snowstorm, gale or fog.

Chapter 6

Putting theory into practice –
the big day out

You have your ferrets and equipment, know how to use it and have permission to ferret, so how do these creatures work – or more importantly how can you understand how they work? There is only one true way to tell, and that's to go ferreting.

The basics of working a ferret are the same for whatever form of ferreting you have decided to participate in, whether the ferret is being shot over, have a dog or hawk waiting for the bolting rabbits or the warren is being netted, the ferret works the same below ground, its job is to persuade the rabbits to bolt. It is just the reactions of the rabbit, due to action and noise above, that the methods to catch the fleeing rabbit are different

The whole aim of ferreting is for the ferret to evict (bolt) the rabbit from its warren.

The rabbit is classed as pest specie, but one with a difference. The classic example of why an animal is classed as a pest – and being in the wrong place at the wrong time is all it takes. Put the rabbit in a nice hutch at the bottom of the garden and it is a popular pet. This is one fact the vast majority of the public finds hard to come to terms with. That is why it is important that ferreting is carried out effectively, humanely, efficiently and safely at all times.

Surveillance is essential to ensure the day runs as smoothly as possible. Having taken a look at the ground that is about to be worked a number of questions are raised. If nets are to be used, will you need to trim the entrances of the warren in advance? Ensure enough nets are taken or use the long nets. Will you need extra help ferreting?

If you are using a hawk or a dog this will bear little relevance; but if you are shooting you will have to think about the safety of both ferrets and the people who are shooting.

Guns present must be 101% safe and aware of the difference between ferret and rabbit. Come to think of it, if they can't tell the difference then they shouldn't be there in the first place! There is no place for an unsafe gun in any day's shooting, not just ferreting. But as we are talking ferreting I will leave the guns out of it. Shooting over ferrets is a very popular method of ferreting but the noise sometimes drives the rabbits to face the ferret below ground as opposed to fleeing freely to face the wrath of the gun.

Check your equipment as there is nothing worse than getting ready to ferret or indeed getting halfway through the day just to realise that a vital piece of equipment has either been left at home or doesn't work. Ferret collars and receivers must be checked; it is always handy to have some spare batteries to hand.

On the morning of the day's ferreting, box up the ferrets that are going to be used ensuring that they are not hungry. They don't need to gorge themselves though otherwise they will only want to sleep. These ferrets will need all their energy; there's a lot of work to be done today.

The day is planned, farmers/landowners and ferreting partners informed and ferrets ready. For the day's ferreting we will be using both nets, purse and long, just to be safe, as these are the most common ways of ferreting
.

Having packed the essential flask, biscuits, ferrets and equipment we set off for the day's sport. The area to be controlled today is a field containing some steep ditches and shrubs/woodland borders.

Upon arrival we take a walk around with the dog to see not only if there are any sitting rough but to send the remainder below ground. (To ferret them out they first need to be below ground.) We will be using the nets first in the ditch. When we use the nets on a day like this it is always useful to have long netted the area just in case there is an undiscovered bolthole.

This is just my preference, others use lurchers only, and others just look and curse themselves for missing that dreaded bolthole.

Before the ferrets can be entered all the holes must be netted, clearing any debris as quietly as possible. It is best to put the bag of nets over your shoulder so they are there for you. This cuts the disturbance on top of the warren to a minimum.

The nets are set over the holes as follows. Pull the unravelled net out by pulling the rings apart to set the net place the bottom ring (opposite to the ring nearest the peg) inside the hole, placing the net over the hole and peg it down securely. The aim is for the rabbit to run over the bottom ring and into the net, the net then purses and the rabbit is caught.

The most common mistakes made by the novice when setting nets are the bolt holes being overlooked, the nets not secured strongly enough by the pegs and the nets becoming full of twigs and debris whilst setting them. But this will pass with experience. Sometimes Mother Nature's obstacles hinder the setting of the net – tree trunks, large entrance holes and hard ground. All will test the patience but persevere and it will be worthwhile.

The nets are set, standing dog ready, now all we need is the ferret. Because the warren is about a dozen holes we are using at least a couple of ferrets. On go the collars and these are tested with the receiver just to make sure all is working.

These collars have revolutionised ferreting but can be a major pain when using nets with large ferrets. The collar, because of the transmitter protruding out makes it hard for the ferret to pass through the net without disturbing it. Some ferrets acquire this knack but the bigger hobs find it hard, though by no means impossible.

Entering a Ferret to a warren

When entering the ferret, find a nice entrance hole that slopes slightly, not one with a steep drop. Your aim if using novice ferrets is to make it as much fun as possible. They have an instinct to explore – just imagine the shock they receive when encountering a rabbit for the first time – be prepared for this. If your homework has been done this will not be a problem, just simply calm the ferret down and let it re-enter the warren at its own pace, do not force it down at any cost.

The ferrets are now working and hopefully a rabbit will appear soon, but you will have to be careful. Rats, stoats, little owls, cats, foxes and birds can all be underground so there is a chance of something unusual being bolted into or through your purse net.

The beauty of purse nets is that if any animals were to be bolted you could set them free and no damage is done. Bear this in mind if your ferrets flatly refuse to enter a burrow – the ferret knows best. If it is the ferrets' first season they will be a little bit excited, tail fluffed out like a bottle cleaner, but all that hard work you've done in handling/socialising when they were kits will pay off. It just takes time and a little patience.

Some time has passed, no ferrets and no rabbits. The ferret has surfaced for a second and then continued working. When the ferret surfaces and takes a quick look outside without leaving the burrow it is usually a sign that there is something down there but refusing to play ball and bolt!

If there were nothing down there the ferrets would surface continually with little enthusiasm to go back down so this is a good sign.

As the receiver box was about to be deployed the silence was broken and after several unmistakable thumps heard under our feet, a rabbit burst out of a hole. Was it netted or did we miss a bolt hole will it escape ?

It was netted. The rabbit lying motionless enclosed in a perfectly pursed net, guarded by my lurcher bramble until I can get there.

Bramble marking a hole, sensing an imminent bolt

Note Brambles quick reaction to the rabbits head emerging from the hole

Bramble reacts to the bolting rabbit, then backs off when she knows the net has done it's job!

Rabbit caught in purse net

Now this animal has to be dispatched, and quickly. There are two methods of dispatching the rabbit and both need to be taught by an experienced hand if you are a newcomer to the sport. The chop method is as the name implies. A sharp blow to the neck by either a priest or your hands will kill the rabbit immediately, but this is a little hit and miss and tends to bruise the meat or just knock out the rabbit so you place it down just for it to recover and escape. The other method is a bit harder but more effective. Take hold of the rabbit either by the midriff or legs and place your thumb behind the rabbit's neck, stretch its body and at the same time push the heads backwards. This will break the neck and death is instant and humane. *See photographs.*

When dealing with a rabbit in the net remember that the hole is now unprotected. Stick your foot in the hole to prevent any rabbit from escaping while you are dealing with the net, or quickly dispatch the rabbit, unpeg the net, place it on the ground and reset a new net and then untangle the dead rabbit when you have time, it's your choice.

When the rabbits are removed from the net don't just chuck them in a pile but empty the bladder. You can do this by holding the rabbit up by its shoulders and feel down the stomach towards the rear end. This will then empty the bladder and this means the meat will not be tainted by the urine. Then place them in a row ready for transporting, or you could leg them. Get hold of one of the rear legs and cut a slot behind the tendon, then place the other leg through this slot. The rabbit can then be carried on a stick. This is invaluable when a big bag is achieved and carrying is made easier by legging the catch. If at the end of the day you catch a lot of rabbits and have a bit of a hike back to your car you may find it easier to gut the rabbits into a large hole, remembering to fill it in, and you would be surprised just how much of the weight is reduced by removing the guts.

After a flurry of rabbits bolting, one of which was caught in the long net because of an overlooked bolthole, the ferrets started to surface and they were picked up and boxed. If a ferret refuses to leave the entrance of a hole, playing the fool at the entrance, this can lead to skulking, but with novices it is just inexperience and should become less of a problem if given the time to come clear of the holes without being scooped up at the first opportunity. Although not unusual for the novice ferret it is an annoying habit that must be broken. Usually you can coax out the ferret with a dead rabbit or a drink of milk from the car, if it is handy, but this must be the last resort. Don't get your ferrets in the habit of having to be bribed out of the holes, someday you might run out of things to bribe it with. Time and patience should do the trick. Do not let frustration beat you and attempt to drag the ferret out – this will only make matters worse.

All but one of the ferrets has been accounted for. After a quick search with the receiver box the rogue animal was found, three feet down. The ferret has laid up. This is either because the ferret has killed below ground and has stuck with the rabbit, or stuck behind the rabbit or, as is common, the rabbit has reached one of its stops. This is a tunnel with a dead end. The rabbit will squeeze into this and stick its rear end out at the ferret. But because the ferret is doing what comes natural it is trying to kill it. (Ferreting can be full of contradictions, for example we want the ferret to bolt the rabbit, and the ferret wants to do the natural instinctive action and kill it.) The ferret will then stay with the rabbit and try to get around the rabbit. The ferret will then have flecks of rabbit fur on its claws, these must be cleaned every time it comes out otherwise you may think it has encountered a rabbit when it hasn't.

A dig will be needed, out comes your friend, the spade.

When the digging commences you must remember that what comes out, you will have to put back. Nothing does more damage to any country sport than the sight of ignorance, and in the past too many ferreters have been refused permission through these actions. Start the dig in the centre of the located spot and dig. Keep the receiver box on just in case the ferret moves. When you are about a half a foot away get the probe and feel for the burrow. This tool makes the finding much quicker and safer for the ferret. Before you have broken through bear in mind the whereabouts of the ferret as it can be easy to break through and decapitate the ferret below.

Once you have broken through you should be on top of the ferret. Pick it up, clean its feet of fur and retrieve the rabbit. After this check the void for another as it has been known for up to six rabbits to be in one dead end. The most I have found is four but a couple is not that uncommon. Now that both rabbit and ferret are retrieved the hole can now be filled in and you can move on to another warren.

Now the nets will need to be picked up, folded and put back in your bag. The rest of the holes will be ferreted using the long nets only and we surrounded the warren completely with a 75-yard net leaving plenty of room for the dog and us humans to operate in and catch and dispatch the fleeing rabbits.

If you do go shooting bolting rabbits safety must come first, for both the ferret and the people around the guns. If the people shooting the rabbits aren't used to the surroundings nothing will be more tempting than the bolting rabbit. When shooting rabbits with ferrets you can cover almost any type of terrain, be it open ground or thick hedgerows or woodlands. The standing guns must be placed at strategic points so they can shoot the rabbits safely without risking ferret or human life. This is sometimes tested when shooting either side of a thick hedge, that is why it is vital everyone is 101% safe and will listen to the person in charge of the ferrets.

The actual working of ferrets is the same as described earlier but without the nets. When shooting though, you tend to see fewer clean bolts into the open and more hole-to-hole bolts. Accidents do happen, but 99% of them can be avoided. It is no good afterwards saying that you thought the polecat ferret was a rabbit in the undergrowth. You must be certain otherwise you shouldn't be there in the first place.

When working your ferrets there might be a time when luck runs out and one of your ferrets goes missing. Many methods can be used to find the ferret – blocking all but one hole, digging a pit for the ferret to fall in and become trapped, or placing the carrying box at the open hole. The method I suggest, although (touch wood) I have never had to use it, is the box-trap method. One of the warreners in Norfolk devised a box similar to a cage trap but with solid sides and a caged window on top. This was devised so when the ferret enters it steps on the step and the door shuts. The ferret will readily enter because it is dark inside. It is caught by its curiosity. This device is used a lot on the estate due to the ferrets being worked in groups of anything up to fifty ferrets and the ferrets are always caught up.

The numbers of working ferrets differs enormously, from a single ferret, a pair of ferrets right up to 50. Whether all with collars or all loose and either a liner or a collared liner depends on the scale of land, rabbits and time allocated to ferreting.

This is the beauty of ferreting, experience will teach you which method suits you best – have faith and patience.

The end of another day's ferreting

Chapter 7

The return home

Upon arrival to your nice warm home, fingers tingling with nettle stings gained during your quest to control the rabbits on your land before jumping into that warm bath with a hot or stiff drink to ponder over the day's actions, haven't you forgot something?

Your ferrets, and possibly dogs, have worked hard today. Take the ferrets to their housing, check for obvious injuries, and feed and water them before turning your attentions to your dog. Dogs I find are good at making you look like a liar in front of the better half later that night. Check over her and remove any thorns that have penetrated her coat. Check her feet - are her pads ok for instance? Dogs, just like us humans, usually don't feel the effects of the day's ferreting until later when the adrenaline has stopped racing around our bodies.

The equipment too cannot wait until morning, or the one after. The ferret finder and collars need to be cleaned and batteries removed ready for another day. Take good care of these sets and they will serve you well, after all they are only as good as the batteries inside them! Leaving the batteries in only reduces their working life and accuracy as a low battery will give a false mark and one that appears deeper than it is - an easy way to miss rabbits or injure your ferret whilst digging.

Your nets, be they hemp, knotless or nylon will need stretching out to dry, especially hemp. This material is probably the best for purse nets in my view but requires that extra bit of attention to ensure the rabbit doesn't waltz through them on your next day out. Nothing could be worse than to get to your ferreting ground only to open up your kit bag to find your nets stuck together and rotting, as well as your ferret finder containing flat or low batteries.

These jobs may take that little bit longer but they are worth it and once you get in the habit of doing them they are then done without thinking about it.

Don't forget that both the ferret and dog uses an enormous amount of energy and courage during a day's ferreting. The best way to ensure you have their company for many a year yet is to give them the best care and attention possible on your return home - no, all the time as it is the little things in life that make the difference.

The author marching at the Liberty & Livelihood march in London on the 22nd September 2002.

Chapter 8

The forgotten meat

No ferreting book would be complete with out a section dedicated to the care of your catch. How many rabbits you catch and what you do with them varies – is it the butcher, game dealer or do you keep them for your own cooking skills to transform them into a tasty meal fit for a king? We must not forget that many in this country relied on rabbit meat during and after two wars. Unfortunately myxomatosis seemed to dampen the appetites since then as well as the thought of picturing what they eat. But it doesn't stop them from eating a chicken, lamb, pig or cow does it? Today's rabbit is as healthy as ever, back with a vengeance and affected little by the scourge of myxomatosis.

The only change is that the harvest of rabbits is today virtually worthless instead of being eagerly awaited as a valuable source of food and income. It cannot be through nutrition. The fact that rabbit meat has more protein and less fat content than pork, lamb, beef or poultry, which, in today's health conscious marketplace, makes it an ideal food. It cannot be through versatility as you can use rabbit as a main ingredient for any recipe that uses meat as its main ingredient, and it isn't hard to get, or at least shouldn't be.

The large majority of people eat from the supermarket and they in turn only stock what people want, sending the little local butcher out of business. But these butchers are one of the few places where you can still obtain wild British rabbit, not the imported stuff at supermarkets.

Whether you want to make a delicious burger, stir-fry it or make a pie, the rabbit is there among the other meats as far as health and versatility are concerned. The following few pages are dedicated to the rabbit as a food source and the reason it reached our shores all those years ago with the Normans.

Convenience is the name of the game today. In the 1950s 30% of the weekly income was spent on food, today that is a mere 10% and with the trend for eating out or pre-cooked meals, 50% of food consumed is either eaten out or prepared outside the kitchen. Surely the time has come in these organically minded days to welcome the rabbit back into our homes as meat to be readily consumed. We don't have to revert to farming them; we have enough of them causing havoc all over the country.

Younger rabbits and does make better eating as the old and bucks tend to be made of a little harder substance. Netted rabbits are far superior as they are clean and are not full of pellets as are rabbits that have been shot –sometimes these are only good for ferret food.

So, please remember all of you out there, the forgotten meal and be a bit adventurous and try the forgotten meat of Britain – the wild rabbit.

A lot of people, myself included, tend to gut the rabbits on site if there is a quantity. To do this you must first ensure that you have dug a big hole, as the neighbours won't be too happy with you after their dog has regurgitated the afternoon's waste all over the kitchen floor!

There are a number of ways you can gut and skin a rabbit but they all finish with the same results, some are just easier and quicker than others. As mentioned earlier it is important to thumb the urine out of the rabbit before gutting, preferably as soon as the rabbit is dispatched as this taints the meat. Some prefer to gut a warm rabbit but many prefer a cool rabbit as it is less messy. Always leave your rabbits out of the direct sunlight if possible, even in the winter as the sun can keep the bodies warm.

To gut the rabbits the easy way, if legged, pull the back legs apart, hold the back legs in one hand upright, I tend to hold the rabbits ears under one foot to give me that little bit of tension. Make a small incision into the fur in the centre the underside of the rabbit an inch or two in front of the back legs and continue to slit through the skin until reaching the front of the rib cage cavity. Another way is to slit the fur in the same place without puncturing the skin and pull the fur apart so you can see what you are doing.

When cutting through the skin use only the tip of a sharp knife ensuring the internal organs are not punctured. With your fingers, or knife, ease out the guts. These will drop towards the floor and your paper/bag which they will be wrapped up in to be disposed of. The guts will drop and the only thing stopping them falling out completely are a few tubes, scoop these out with your knife or hand.

The rabbit has now been gutted, now for the skin.

Get your sharp knife, or it is easier with a pair of good clean secateurs, and chop off the feet just below the first joint and at the neck, this takes off the head. Simply get hold off the fur in the middle of the body and pull apart, the fur will head towards the rear legs and the front likewise. Split this fur in two to make life easier. As you have removed the feet the fur will pull over these areas leaving a freshly gutted and skinned rabbit, ready for you to cook, freeze or sell.

The recipes listed below are subject to regional differences but signify the three ways in which we eat – burger, casserole and barbecue. I cannot be there with you so therefore I cannot be responsible if your cooking is as bad as my shooting, but remember that rabbit can substitute any meat used as a main ingredient for almost any meal.

The Bunny Burger

 2lb of minced rabbit meat
3 chopped tomatoes
1 finely chopped onion or leek
A small pinch of rosemary
3 chopped rashers of bacon
2 teaspoons of mixed herbs
A dash of Worcestershire sauce
A dash of tomato sauce
A tablespoon of pickle
2 fresh eggs
Bread crumbs to bind the mixture,
usually I use 1 pint but each individual
may add or subtract any amount.

The above are mixed thoroughly and pressed into shape either using a burger maker or by weighing a ¼ pound at a time and pressing. You may want to make them as thick or thin as you like.

Rabbit casserole
Serves 4

2oz butter
1 jointed rabbit
2 peeled and chopped onions
Salt and pepper
1 tablespoon of flour
3/4 pint of stock
2 tablespoons of tomato puree
Large pinch of mixed herbs

Place the jointed the rabbit into some freshly melted butter in a pan, fry briskly until browned. Place in casserole dish adding the onions and salt and pepper to taste.

Stir the flour into pan and cook for a couple of minutes, constantly stirring the contents.

Stir in the stock and bring to the boil and simmer for 2-3 minutes stirring in the tomato puree and mixed herbs. Pour contents over rabbit, cover and cook for 1½ to 2 hours at gas mark 4 or 350f/280c.

Barbecue Rabbit

Joint your rabbit and soak for 25 minutes in a salted water/ herb mix. Drain and dry. Roll meat in some melted butter ensuring a good even coat. Roll in some breadcrumbs and cook on your barbeque.

Chapter 9

Summary

There we have it, a few pages hopefully helping and not hindering your start in ferreting and a few tips that have served me well.

But what about the future for your ferreting? Before putting this book down, just think what the future might have in store for you and your newly acquired or usual pastime. The following three passages may, in my view, help all of our futures.

Ferreting is just one of many country pursuits, or field sports as they are called, and although not as high profile as hunting, shooting or fishing, nevertheless it still is one. In the politically correct obsessed world we are fast becoming, the knives are out by those who either genuinely fail to understand these activities or are just ignorant about them We must never let ferreting, or ferreting with the aid of dogs, to become embroiled in such legislation. Never pass at the opportunity to express yourself to explain just how and why you do what you do. You are proud of your ferrets and ferreting, never become afraid or ashamed to admit it and don't let anyone take that proud feeling away from you.

Because the ferret has now become such a popular pet we are experiencing the same difficulties the dog world has experienced before us, namely we humans changing the set-up of our animals to suit our obsessions. To ensure the ferret does not continue down this road as, for example, the Springer spaniel – one show type and another to fulfil a day's work but both the same breed. Because we are now showing ferrets, Mr or Mrs Jones wants something different, to win a rosette with, we then take the ferret from its origins and meddle with nature for different colours, size and shape.

There is absolutely nothing wrong in breeding your own ferrets for your needs, but to work your ferret requires a mind and body fit for such a role. To show, an animal needs to look good. The working ferret can do both, but can the show ferret work as nature intended? The majority can, but get a few generations down the line and the hunting gene is no longer needed. Instinct to explore every nook and cranny, and ability and tolerance are all the qualities that have helped the ferret become such a popular creature be it to work or keep as a pet, or both. We must never forget just why we domesticated the ferret all those years ago – to work.

And finally, after ensuring you can ferret, and with ferrets that want to work, make sure there are people out there who are as equally willing to go ferreting. They are our future, for without them we will just become another bygone of the countryside.

Useful contacts

These contacts will enable you to get equipment, books, videos and regular magazines on the subject. The Countryman's Weekly is especially good for ferret and lurcher enthusiasts.

Organisations

British Association for Shooting & Conservation
Marford Mill, Rossett, Wrexham LL12 0HL
www.basc.org.uk

Countryside Alliance
367 Kennington Road, London SE11 4PT
www.countryside-alliance.org

The Game Conservancy Trust
Fordingbridge, Hampshire SP6 1EF

Union of Country Sports Workers
P.O. Box 129, Banbury, Oxfordshire OX17 2HX
www.ucsw.org

Association of Lurcher Clubs
c/o Alan Tyer Tel: 01617 640958 or Paul Saiger Tel: 01913 779122

Ferreting Association for the Control of Rabbits
Tel: 023 8087 3381

National Ferret Welfare Society
113 Henry Street, Kenilworth, Leamington Spa, Warwickshire CU8 2HL

Ferreting equipment

Pakefield Ferrets – makers of traditional bowback ferret carrying boxes.
Events, educational & ferreting days, rabbit control etc
Tel: 01502 568571 Mobile:07766 168817
www.pakefieldferrets.co.uk

Deben Group Industries Ltd
Deben Way, Melton, Woodbridge, Suffolk IP12 1RS
Tel: 0870 4422600
www.deben.com

Attlebrough Accessories
Morley St Peter, Wymondham, Norfolk NR18 9TZ
Tel: 01953 454932
www.attac.com

Ian Hodge Fieldsports
Wadebridge, Cornwall PL27 7LA
Tel: 01208 813652

Coch-y-Bonddu Books
Pentrehedyn Street, Machynlleth, Powys SY20 8DJ
Tel: 01654 702837
www.anglebooks.com

Tideline Books
Tideline House, 49 Kinmel Street, Rhyl, Denbighshire LL18 1A9
Tel: 01745 354919
www.tidelinebooks.co.uk

Bridport Nets
Unit 5, Old Timber Yard, West Bay, Bridport, Dorset DT6 4EL
Tel: 01308 420927

Brian Brinded Rabbit Longnets & Accessories
Cedarwood, Raydon Rd, Bacons Green, Holton St.Mary, CO7 6NJ
Tel: 01473 310704 Mobile:07768 008863

Ferret Food Manufacture

Chudleys Ferret:Dodson & Horrell Ltd

Chudleys Ferret has been uniquely formulated to provide the ferret with all the necessary nutrients required for a working life. Suitable for all types of ferret including kits and adult ferrets.
If you would like further information on Chudleys ferret food then please contact our Helpline on 0870 442 3322 or visit our web-site
www.chudleys.co.uk

Sporting Press

Countryman's Weekly
Yelverton, Devon PL20 7PE
Tel: 01822 855281

Shooting Times & Country Magazine, Sporting Gun
Room 2107, Kings Reach Tower, Stamford Street, London SE1 9LS
Tel: 0207 261 5069

Shooting Gazette
Bourne Publishing Group Ltd, Roebuck House, 33 Broad Street, Stamford, Lincolnshire PE9 1RB
Tel: 01780 754900

Index